Advance Praise for *Men are Pigs*

"Sturgeon takes the same 'no BS' attitude that has made him a successful businessman and applies it to dating, sex, and marriage."

—McKenzie Smith, Dallas TX

"Few speak about the differences between the sexes or the real desires of men. Sturgeon does both without apology. I'm glad someone is finally saying this stuff!"

—Greg Morse, President of a Texas bank, published author

"Every woman should read this book! Reading it and acting on the advice will make any relationship stronger."

—Kristy Remo, Fort Worth Entrepreneur

"A high-five for men and a revelation for women, this book will help both get luckier in bed, courtship, and marriage."

—Josh Davis, Web Consultant, Made In Fort Worth.com

"Ron tells it like it is. If a woman is offended, it's because she isn't in the 20 percent who love sex. That's fine, as long as she finds a man who also doesn't love sex."

—Jonna Downey, Weatherford Texas

"Wow. This is must-read for those who want long lasting relationships."

—Brian Nerney, Seattle Washington

MEN ARE
PIGS
AND THAT'S A GOOD THING

MEN ARE
PIGS
AND THAT'S A GOOD THING

9 Secrets and 7 Strategies
to get more women, steamier sex,
and better relationships

INCLUDES
THE HOLY GRAIL—
27 Ways to Spot Women Who *Really* Need Sex

RON STURGEON

Mission Impossible Publishing
Fort Worth
2014

Published by

Mission Possible Publishing
P.O. Box 37007
Haltom City, Texas 76117

For more information, contact Jennifer Knittel at
Jenniferk@rdsinvestments.com or
817-834-3625, Ext. 232

Copyright © 2014 Ron Sturgeon
First edition: January 2014

For reseller information including quantity discounts and bulk sales, please contact the publisher.

ISBN: 978-0-9851112-1-2
Manufactured in the United States of America
10 9 8 7 6 5 4 3 2 1
First Edition

To Linda,
my wonderful life mate.
I hope she will tolerate me forever.

CREDITS AND ACKNOWLEDGMENTS

WRITER
Mark Stuertz

PROJECT MANAGER
Eric Anderson

EDITORS
Eric Anderson, Jonna Downey, Linda Allen
Mike Goodrich, Kristy Remo, Mark Wood, Adam Hicks
Steve Migues, Greg Morse, Debra Pope, Brian Nerney

COVER DESIGNS
Ron Sturgeon & 99 Designs

ADVISORS
Brian Judd, Dan Poynter, Mark Stuertz,
Eric Anderson, Paula Felps, Cindy Baldoff

ILLUSTRATORS
Dug Nap & Gahan Wilson

PUBLISHER
Mission Possible Publishing

Special thanks to my "consumer testing group," the dozens of friends
and colleagues who voted, edited, and advised on everything from
book design to the marketing campaign.

Contents

Foreword

D epending on your vantage point, the "men are pigs" cliché either elicits comfort, resignation, or fury. In this book, Ron Sturgeon attempts to unleash all three at once—a whack on the side of the head to dislodge your preconceived notions on sex and relationships. And get you out of your romantic rut. Does it work? You be the judge.

I first became acquainted with Sturgeon while I was a staff writer at the *Dallas Observer*, where I was a feature and food and wine critic. I would regularly get press releases from the DFW Elite Toy Museum, a collection of some 3,000 rare and unique toys and miniature cars. Those were followed by releases extolling another Sturgeon creation: the DFW Elite Auto Club. The Auto Club was a fractional ownership program where, via a monthly fee, you could tool around in a Bentley Continental GT, a Ferrari F430 F1, or a Porsche 911 Cabriolet over a different weekend each month.

A couple of years ago he sent me a copy of his book *Getting to Yes With Your Banker*, a collection of tips (making lunch count) and traps in banking relationships. He also reveals in *Getting to Yes* that one of his Auto Club clients cut a bright green Lamborghini in half with a tree, giving new meaning to the term *fractional ownership*.

Ron Sturgeon is a serial entrepreneur, one with seemingly boundless energy and creativity. Yet his passions aren't diffused. They're focused primarily on what he calls automobilia, reflecting a zeal for piston toys in all sizes and guises.

A few months after receiving his book, I got an email from Sturgeon. He was looking for a collaborator on a book he was composing on sex and relationships. Paula Felps, a colleague of mine who worked with Sturgeon on many of his other books, suggested I might be a good fit because of my interest in cars. Plus I enjoyed modest success with erotic fiction in the mid-1990s and she thought these sensibilities might come in handy. I was intrigued.

More intriguing than that was how Sturgeon came upon the idea for the book. Fresh from a divorce, he began dating and talking to other singles on the agonies and ecstasies of meeting people and forming and maintaining lasting relationships. Through these conversations, Sturgeon began noticing consistencies in the stories he was hearing from both men and women.

Unlike many who have attempted to tackle the issue, Sturgeon is a fearless and effective interrogator. He honed the process by devising a list of standard questions to tease out perceptions many people unknowingly keep under wraps. He collected and organized these stories over a period of four years. The result is *Pigs*, a brash, seat-of-the-pants study on men and women and what happens when they make contact.

Pigs is informal, laced with Sturgeon's edgy, off-the-grid interpretations, commentary, and advice. To say it's an unexpected detour for an all-business, nuts and bolts entrepreneur like Sturgeon is an understatement. (Sturgeon tracks his credit rating like other men track box scores.)

His story is a classic rags-to-riches tale. When Sturgeon was a teenager working his way through high school as a grocery store produce manager, his father died suddenly. His stepmother kicked him and his twin brother out of the house. All he had to his name was a 1965 Volkswagen Beetle and $2,000 his father had left him for college. He had nowhere to live and a Volkswagen to share.

But he had an idea. In 1973, he teamed up with a friend whose father owned and operated an automotive glass shop. They launched a Volkswagen repair business by renting one of the service bays. AAA Bug Service was born.

A year later, he obtained a dealer's license and began accumulating wrecked cars for parts. Before long, he was making more money selling parts from those wrecks than he was repairing cars in running condition. So he opened a junkyard with one employee.

Junk was good to Ron Sturgeon. Or maybe Ron Sturgeon was good to junk. In 1985 he designed a rudimentary computer program on an Apple IIe to manage his salvage yard inventories and maximize profits. With this system, Sturgeon could accurately predict exactly which parts on a specific vehicle would sell. He scrapped the rest.

Seven years later he opened a second salvage yard, moving into highline vehicles with nameplates such as BMW, Mercedes, and Lexus. It was while working with these nameplates that he developed an innovative database driven direct-mail marketing program—highly unusual for a junkyard. Sturgeon was sending out some 1 million direct mail pieces per year, cross referencing calls to a series of 800 numbers with zip codes to determine which areas were yielding the best returns. His strategy caught the eye of *INC* magazine, which profiled Sturgeon and his innovative direct-mail program in June 1994.

Five years later, Sturgeon sold AAA Small Car World— one of the largest auto recyclers in the nation—to Ford Motor Company. Price: somewhere north of $10 million. In 2001 he left Ford to launch an auto auction for insurers. A year later he sold the venture for more than $5 million in stock to the largest publicly held company in the sector.

Then in 2003, Sturgeon bought back his auto recycling business from Ford. The company had grown from six locations in Texas with 150 employees and $15 million in sales, to 30 locations in 19 states with 1,000 employees and $140 million in sales.

The company was also drowning in red ink. Sturgeon worked doggedly with his partners for 18 months wringing out inefficiencies. He returned the company to profitability.

He and a pair of partners sold it to Schnitzer Industries in 2005 for millions. He and his junk hit pay dirt again.

These days, Sturgeon consults, gives speeches as Mr. Mission Possible, and oversees a swath of commercial real estate totaling some one million square feet. And he writes books.

So what does proficiency with scrap fenders and valve covers have to do with romance and knowing when to touch the small of a woman's back? Nothing. And everything. Sturgeon has spent his life wrestling with conundrums, analyzing everything he came into contact with. And what are sex and romance if not the mother of all conundrums?

If business and entrepreneurship teaches anything, it's that cost-benefit analysis must be applied to all areas of life if you're going to enjoy success and happiness. And great sex. If benefits exceed costs, it's best to continue investing in—and working—the process. Once that equation flips, cut your losses and move on. It's birds and bees 101—from the point of view of a spreadsheet.

Sturgeon says his greatest talent is the ability to make complex things simple. Which is not the same as making hard things easy. He also has a knack for taking successful processes he discovers from other businesses and applying them to his own ventures. To paraphrase Picasso: Creative people borrow. It takes a genius to steal.

Pigs is a blunt, entertaining and no-holds-barred peek into the explosive chemistry of sex and romance—from a seldom discussed perspective. And—in the current social orthodoxy where the feminine is idealized while the masculine is scoffed at—a refreshing take in its brazen political incorrectness. So proceed at your own risk. You'll either throw this book at the wall or highlight a few excerpts and frame and hang them there.

—*Mark Stuertz*

Introduction

*M*en are Pigs. It's hard to think of three words that are more insulting when describing the friction between men and women. Women think men are pigs because all they think about is sex. Men think women are pigheaded because they refuse to see the importance of sex. It's the *elephant-in-the-room* between the sexes. This disconnect can poison and wreck a relationship. You can't wish away the differences between men and women, no matter how "enlightened" you may think such wishing might be. But if you learn how a pig thinks and what motivates him, you can make him dance at will.

I originally wanted to call this book *Pedestal Treatment*. It was to be a collection of simple strategies to keep marital bonds warm. I wondered: what would happen if you got out of bed every morning and asked your spouse "What can I do to keep you one more day?"

As a serial entrepreneur in my 50s, I have had a long run of business successes (plus a few failures). My friends say that I'm obsessive compulsive. Others say I'm anal. But everyone agrees my success is due in large part to a knack for analyzing business experiences and learning the right lessons from them. I applied these same skills to this book. So my approach is different from most writers who publish books of this sort. It's a collection of experiences gathered from interviews exploring the triumphs and pitfalls of sex and relationships.

I began by interviewing only men. As you can imagine a lot of men my age are divorced (many are re-married). So I got some pretty good stories describing the ebb and flow of long-term relationships. And what happens when things go wrong. I heard over and over about menopause, for example. Soon I began interviewing women.

In the early stages of my research, it became clear that this book was not going to be about how to stay married. Something else popped up. This was exciting because I realized another book on how to stay married would just be one in about 6,312 other books on the same subject. This book was going to stand out from that pack.

I couldn't believe what I discovered. The stories women and men tell are basically the same. When you talk to men they say "Oh my God. All women are liars. They're cheats. They've got baggage. They blow my phone up with texts. They're high maintenance." When you talk to women they say, "Oh my God. All men are scoundrels. They're cheats. They blow up my phone with texts. They're needy." It's the same list.

Introduction

But as I dug deeper, clear differences began to appear. My first revelation was that God really did wire men and women differently. Strange that this should be a revelation. Many in "polite society" and far too many women are in denial of this fact. All of the men claimed they weren't getting enough sex. All of the women claimed they were providing their men with plenty of sex. That's one huge disconnect.

Fact: men want sex. Fact: most women simply don't care all that much about sex, at least not in the same way or to the same degree as men. Not even close. Yet strangely, most of the men I interviewed claimed they had been—at one time or another—with a woman who needed sex. Not wanted sex, *needed* sex. Regularly. There was something different about that woman, these men told me. She had a certain way about her.

That's when I discovered the *Holy Grail*. What's the Holy Grail? It's a set of traits and behaviors that women who truly need sex display at one time or another—as revealed by the happy men who experienced them. They're real. I didn't make them up.

Think of the Holy Grail as a field guide for picking out women with huge sexual appetites from the more sexually inhibited crowd—if that's to your liking. If you want relationships rocked by mind-blowing sex on a regular basis—to whatever degree of intensity your heart desires (or can withstand)—be assured that there's a woman out there for you.

But once you find her, you still have to keep her. That's why this book has a practical piece with tips on how to make your relationships better. *Pigs* even includes its own token or medallion system—similar to the reminder systems used in many successful treatment and self-help regimens—to help you develop habits that will keep both of you coming back for more. For years. If you can stand it.

My second revelation was that people will tell you the darnedest things—*if you ask them*. It's amazing how blasé many of us are about the world around us. No wonder we get bored with one another. Our lack of curiosity essentially creates a highly profitable jobs program for couples counselors and divorce lawyers. Maybe this book will make them less necessary.

I also discovered Pretty Girl Syndrome, the existence of cell phones with selective text and voice options (STVO) synchronized to female (and sometimes male) fickleness, why women hate performing oral sex, and how to determine where a woman ranks on the scale of sexual interest, etc., etc.

Early reviews of my findings from friends, colleagues, and editors were encouraging—if polarizing can be considered encouraging. Comments ranged from "damn right, all men are rapist pigs" to "wow, glad to see someone is actually talking about this stuff" and "the Holy Grail is so cool."

I gathered the information for this book over a 4-year period, conducting hundreds of interviews with scores of men and women aged twenty-something to sixty-something. This book was written by a man—it's from a man's perspective. It's not a scientific or formal research study. It's simply a record of conversations.

I tried to be objective, and I certainly got a lot of feedback from women. Yet the musk of male temperament saturates these pages. (If you want a book from a female perspective, there are plenty of those out there.)

The result will educate, entertain, and perhaps even repulse you. You likely won't agree with everything I say in these pages. And that's okay. Because if we all had the same tastes, we'd all be driving 4-door white Chevys, there'd be only one banker, one type of woman, we'd all be chasing her, and she would really like it. The rest of us would really hate it. Well, the banker might like it. Especially if that banker was a woman.

Oink oink.

CHAPTER 1

How to Find the Right Person

"A man loses his sense of direction after four drinks;
a woman loses hers after four kisses."

— EARLY 20TH CENTURY JOURNALIST AND SATIRIST H.L. MENCKEN

How do you find and meet people? How do you choose the right ones for possible romantic relationships? How difficult is this process? This is a huge topic. Everywhere you go people complain about how challenging it is to meet someone. We assume there are a number of eligible people out there who are just right for us. When it's right, it should be easy. It shouldn't be a struggle. But it is.

Why? We think everybody out there is normal. But there are a lot of people out there who aren't really normal. You meet these people when you're dating.

Almost everyone lies when dating. They tell you money doesn't matter. They try to impress you by saying they own

7

real estate in Pebble Beach. They tell you they absolutely love kids and gourmet cooking. Then you come to find out they're lactose and spice intolerant, they want to know the most you've ever spent on a date, they complain about everyone's kids, and their real estate investments consist of a timeshare in a motel along California Highway 1.

There are a few quick filters you can use so that you don't waste your time. For example, I have a friend who runs his own business and when he interviews potential employees, he sends someone out to the parking lot to peek into their car. If the car is a mess, that's how he expects they will keep their desk. The way a person keeps their car and home is often how they keep themselves. So if this is a red flag for you, be aware of it.

Here's another one: If a woman orders three drinks (or salads) in a row and sends them all back, it's pretty clear she's hard to please. One more: observe how a person salts their food. If they salt their food before they taste it, they may have hard-wired habits and will be resistant to change. Evaluate accordingly.

Most people seem okay—until you spend some time with them. What usually happens is two hours, two days, two weeks, or two months into the relationship, they're not what you thought they were. Things start to surface. Whatever little red flags were waving in the beginning turn into rows of red flashing lights with sirens after a few weeks. When people feel comfortable enough to dial back their best behavior, the warts and boils can come out with a vengeance. To succeed, you have to be smart. And really lucky.

How to Get Lucky

There are so many complications and hazards in the dating game it's enough to make your head spin. Or bobble. First, there's the issue of simply being single, especially if you've been single for a long time. People often get suspicious of long-term singles.

Why? The longer people are single, the more independent they become. They get to be highly protective of their "me space." They lose interest in accommodating others and have little patience for compromise. They've learned to be self-sufficient and they're resistant to change. They get anal and turn pissy if you try to widen their horizons. They're a good fit for someone. It just may not be you.

Of course, older singles have to change somewhat. But the change will be incremental. If you're a displaced travel agent, you're not going to suddenly learn how to become a plumber. You are what you are. Just remember, after about the age of 40, most people are fully set in their ways. And it can be argued that you shouldn't be trying to radically change someone anyway. That doesn't mean they can't be persuaded to compromise and learn new things.

Through my interviews I discovered there are a lot of 40 and 50-year-old divorced women out there who are looking for someone. But one guy told me that after he turned 40, women started dumping him after the first few dates once they found out he had never been married. These women thought there was something wrong with him, that he was defective in some way. The "single" issue can be a problem of both reality and perception.

About the Research

I interviewed several hundred adult men and women from all age groups over a four-year period for this book. At the start, I used the same set of questions for each subject, refining it as I went along. I was amazed at what people will reveal if you just ask and sincerely listen (and those that know me know that I am not afraid to ask—about anything). My interview subjects—both men and women—were willing to talk. They were eager to discuss their own ideas, insights, and experiences—the good and the bad. And they were hungry for solutions—the crux of this book.

But older people have at least one advantage. While older singles may play games, they don't game the dating system as often as younger singles do. Older singles tend to skip the power plays, the teases, the jealousy ploys, the hard-to-get headaches, and the "jumping through hoops" trials to prove worthiness. They simply don't have the time, energy, or willingness. That's why for older singles the weeding process is far more efficient. It can also be lonelier.

Where to Begin?

You can meet people on the Internet, in bars, at the grocery store, at church, in classes, or at work. Obviously you have to be very careful at work. It's filled with professional and legal hazards. As the sayings go: "Don't get your meat where you get your bread" and "Don't dip your pen in the company ink well."

Be creative. Be open to possibility in unexpected places. I talked to one guy who met his long-term girlfriend after selling her a car for her son.

 One good rule of thumb is to regularly participate in things you are passionate about. That way, you have some common ground established and increase your chances of making a solid connection. Yet even with all of these options it's still challenging. So be ready to put some work into it. And be patient.

One thing I came across repeatedly: The 45 to 60-year-old guy who's recently divorced and is dating a girl 20 or more years his junior. Yes, she looks good on the arm. Sure, she's crazy in the sack. But what the hell does he think she is going to want in 20 years when he is all shriveled up?

I met one 50-year-old who was dating a 20-something and he didn't understand why her parents didn't like him.

What? Is he from Mars? All of our ex's think we left them for much younger women. I don't believe that's true in general. But that doesn't mean a few of us won't end up with a spring chicken.

Just keep it real, guys. Keep the age gap to ten years give or take. Granted it isn't easy to find a woman in the forty-something age bracket who is still working her charms to dizzying effect. But she's out there. So don't give up.

Where to Get Lucky

Everybody says, "Oh you never meet anyone worthwhile in a bar." What does that mean? I'm in a bar. You're in a bar. Are we saying that good people don't go to bars? I went to bars because I wanted to meet people. I wanted to meet other people who go to bars to meet people. Everybody says it's a bad idea to try to meet someone in a bar. Yet we all go to bars.

Here's the thing: There are good bars and there are bad bars. There are dives and there are classy spots. Explore. Be selective. Many clubs and organizations have monthly happy hours. Find one suitable and join. It's a great way to sample venues and mingle with prospects. There's a bar out there that fits your style. If you want a classy girl, go to a classy bar. If you want a biker girl, go to a biker bar (and there's nothing wrong with that if that's what you want). So belly up.

Many of the people I interviewed had great success with Internet dating sites. And while there are several sites that are good for establishing relationships, there are also a lot of good sites if you just want to get laid. Match. com seems to be one of those.

A friend of mine who is 50 has three dates a week. He has sex with three different women every week. And it's all

Think College is Endless Sex? Think Again.

Men on college campuses are at risk too. If a female student accuses a male student of sexual assault, the male student is assumed guilty. Colleges and universities now use the lowest possible standard of proof in these cases. This means that if a school thinks there is as little as a 50.001% chance the guy is guilty (a preponderance of evidence instead of the clear and convincing evidence standard), he is assumed guilty and must be disciplined. He can be expelled and face civil and criminal penalties without a fair hearing. At the University of North Dakota, a student was convicted of sexual assault on flimsy evidence by a UND tribunal and was suspended and banned from campus for three years. Three months later the police charged the guy's accuser with filing a false police report, but the university refused to reinstate him—until the warm light of publicity got too hot ("Yes Means Yes—Except on Campus," *Wall Street Journal,* July 15, 2011). Eventually, the sanctions against the male student were dropped.

through one of the big online dating sites. He says a lot of these women are married. They tell him they are estranged from their spouses, but still living with them. Go figure.

Many men dream of living a lifestyle like this, at least for a short time. When they first become single they expect to date and bed multiple women. They imagine getting laid "with different girls at different times" without ever having to make a commitment. And these days, that's more reality than fantasy. Everyone can groupie-up like a rock star in the Internet age.

But in the real world this lifestyle can get difficult to manage. There's no way you can have a girl on Monday, a girl on Wednesday followed by another on Friday, have sex with each, then follow-up in another two weeks, take them out, and have sex with them again. It's not sustainable.

There's also serious danger in this lifestyle—besides the risk of sexually transmitted diseases that is. Two of the men I interviewed who met a woman on dating sites such as Plenty Of Fish or Zoosk had just one date with each. Babies followed a few months later. Now they're paying child support. That's sex they'll never forget.

Fact: Women do lie about being on birth control. Many are not above using paternity claims to set up income streams. And the law is on their side, no matter how flimsy the claims. If a woman accuses you of fathering a child and gets the legal gears in motion, it's almost impossible to turn them off. She is always given the benefit of the doubt. Always.

Avoid the Dangers and High Costs of the Weenie Trap.

Even with DNA evidence, once the government's "dead-beat dad" steamroller gets going, it can cost you years and thousands of dollars in legal bills to prove your seed didn't sprout that kid. And if you do prove it, you won't get any refunds on the child support you were unfairly forced to pay. Some states have passed paternity fraud laws to shield men from this violation of their rights, but most haven't. So protect yourself, both with latex (make sure that *you*, not her, dispose of the spent condom) and a grasp of the legal landscape.

If you want to have sex, you can have lots of it in this age of cyber romance. And men like to have sex. If you want to find a long-term relationship, you can find that too. You just have to be honest with yourself and with those you interact with. And be smart.

Slow is Better Than Fast

I haven't met or interviewed anyone who thought he or she was going to have a meaningful relationship with someone after having sex on the first date. That doesn't mean it doesn't happen, but I believe it's the exception.

 Waiting can be a good strategy. Here's why: Abstinence makes the loins grow fonder. For men, holding back also shows you aren't completely ruled by your pork rind. It also adds a new, unexpected dimension to being aroused.

Kiss and embrace passionately as if you're going to go for the wild thing and then ease back. It'll freak her out. She'll go wild for you. In this instant gratification culture, people forget the blinding power of sexual tension. It's a huge turn-on, especially for women. It's almost as if they prefer anticipation to gratification. When you finally do claw back the sheets, your self control will yield huge returns.

Sex too early brings out too many emotions. It pulls out so many things, most of which you don't necessarily want to experience with someone you've just met. Women tend to get that warm cuddly "Oh my god I think I'm in love" feeling after sex. For men it's more like "Wow. I got off. That was great. Are you ready for some football?"

A good rule of thumb is to wait three or four dates before you take the plunge. Or more. Many men believe in the four-date rule though. If no sex by then, they are done. One man I interviewed had 13 dates before he had sex with the woman he was dating. And they're still going strong four years later. For them 13 is a very lucky number.

Women: if you really don't want to have sex on the first date, make sure you give clear signals. Maybe tell him you're looking for a relationship at the outset and see how he responds. Remind him of that if he gets too frisky. It's a good filter.

Keep the pace leisurely throughout the relationship. It's so easy to pass out keys, codes and gate remotes, for example. And it's so hard to take them back. Why do people feel so driven to give their lover keys to their apartment or the house? It's a metaphor for so many things.

It's the key to your heart—to your life. It's like an ownership document if you will. We offer it because we're trying to draw them in, to keep them. But it's a mistake. You don't have to give away the key—until you're absolutely sure. You'll regret it when you have to ask for it back or change the codes. It's like a divorce. A bad one.

Slow is better than fast. Even for a pig.

CHAPTER 2

How to Determine
Who's Not Wrong

Filters and Deal Breakers

*"I'm not offended by all the dumb blonde jokes because I
know I'm not dumb . . . and I also know that I'm not blonde."*
— DOLLY PARTON

*"Whenever I date a guy, I think, is this the man I want
my children to spend their weekends with?"*
— ACTRESS AND COMEDIENNE RITA RUDNER

We often enter the dating phase trying
to decide who is right for us. We meet
someone. We do our leg sniffs. We're trying to decide if
this is the right person. Or could be.

This is a mistake. We shouldn't be trying to decide if
a person is right for us. It causes too much stress, and can
cause us to prematurely eliminate good prospects. This

is what girls with Pretty Girl Syndrome (PGS) tend to do (see Chapter 3).

 We should be trying to figure out if they're wrong. Or not wrong. If we decide they're not wrong, it doesn't necessarily mean they're right. We need to move from *not wrong* to *might be right*. At that point, we can begin to move to *right*. From there we might cautiously consider if the person could be *The One*.

Yet once we've decided someone is wrong, we shouldn't spend another second with that person. Fully one-third of the women I interviewed were with men they admitted had serious issues. Many of these guys weren't working. Or they drank too much. Or they were irresponsible in money matters, borrowing cash and skipping out on financial obligations. A few of these women told me they stayed with these men because they were trying to fix them.

"I know I'm being stupid about it, but I just love him," one woman admitted to me. I don't think these women understand that it's okay to not love someone who is a jerk. The typical drama plays out like this: She meets him; she has fun with him; she thinks he's cool and exciting. The next thing she knows, she thinks she's in love with him. And then she finds out he's a self-centered jerk.

What she doesn't seem to get is that at this point it's okay not to be in love with him. There's nothing wrong with falling out of love with a jerk. She is probably more

behave
,ll behave
will behave
I will behave
I will behave
I will behave
I will behave

Women Make the Mistake of Thinking They can "Fix" Guys who aren't Worth the Trouble.

in love with the prospect of fixing the jerk than the actual jerk anyway. I found *lots* of women who were acting like mothers, trying to rehab their men. You just want to grab these women and shake them to see if you can unscramble their brains.

And what's with that new couple we all know? They have been together two months and have already broken up once. When we are around them, they snipe and fuss. Trust me. If it's not easy at first, it's not right. Run. Run away. Fast.

After we've decided someone is wrong, he or she should be gone—out of our lives for good. Life is too short.

Deal Breakers and Filters

 The first step in figuring out who's not wrong is to put the person through your own personal screening process: the deal breakers that earn someone the thumbs-down, and the filters that put him or her on notice. We all have our hot button annoyances, whether we admit it or not. Maybe we eliminate the guy who wears briefs, or reconsider the girl who takes forever to apply too much eye makeup.

Most women, for example, will not date a guy who is shorter than they are. By my estimate, some 60 percent of women absolutely will not consider someone whose final growth spurt doesn't clear the top of her hairdo (Tom Cruise doesn't get hit with this deal breaker for some reason).

So God be with you if you're a short man. You've just been eliminated from 60 percent of your potential opportunities. It's a huge problem for these women because there's a great guy out there who is two inches shorter than they are (and maybe two inches longer than they think). We are all the same height in bed anyway.

You will have to decide which items are deal breakers. Make the list short. The rest are filters. Your personal list of deal breakers and filters might include the following (these are not in any particular order—everyone's rankings will be different):

- Race and/or ethnicity (This is much less of an issue among younger people.)
- Religion
- Prejudices
- Smoking
- Political party affiliation/ideology
- Drug use
- Pets
- A criminal record
- Age
- Baggage (Problems with an ex or with kids.)
- Lack of ambition (No aspirations is a big turn off for most.)
- Gold diggers
- Freeloaders & bums (I discovered a lot of the women were dating or had dated men who couldn't hold down a job. They were always broke. Yet these women kept dating them, thinking it was going to get better.)
- Ballooning paunches, multilevel chins, spare tires, thunder thighs, and monster tushes (Many people refuse to date a person who is overweight or is beyond a certain dress size.)
- Sense of entitlement (Younger men and especially younger women seem to have a towering sense of entitlement. Older women may want and expect nice things, but they're far less demanding and more realistic about what a man can reasonably provide.)
- Lack of manners/bad habits (A big turnoff for women: talking while chewing food.)

- Excessive profanity
- Rudeness directed at service people (or anyone else)
- A person who is habitually inconsiderate
- Lack of interest in others (People who always talk about themselves are a bore.)
- Lack of assertiveness
- Bad hygiene
- Credit or financial mismanagement
- Unkempt vehicles
- Baldness (though it can be sexy too!)
- Tattoos or face and body piercings
- Moving too fast toward commitment (Slow is better than fast. We get to know each other better in everything from sex to the dog. If someone attempts to rush commitment with an ultimatum, run.)
- "I love you" (We are much too casual with this four-letter word—we rush into saying it. I have often wished there was a word between like and love. We shouldn't feel pressured to confess love with someone just because we feel stronger than "like." And watch out for the manipulative "I love you" that expects the obligatory "I love you too" response. I personally will never tell a girl I love her *during* sex. It seems obligatory. Instead, make your expression specific: *I love your legs* or *I love the way you walk* or *I love the way you make me feel*.)
- Bad teeth
- Talking too much on the phone (Preoccupation with cell phones is another turn off for many people.)

- Handling work issues that aren't critical after hours
- Annoying friends
- Annoying family (If your lover's parents and siblings don't like you, say hello to misery.)
- Frequently talking about the ex (Mention it and then shut up unless asked. People who constantly talk about their exes are most likely the ones with drama in their lives.)
- Frequently talking about your kids
- Dishonesty
- Lousy in bed
- Too much texting (During the leg-sniffing phase, it's a good idea to limit texting and email until you get to know each other better. It's difficult to pick up on the unspoken assumptions in texts and emails. "Are they kidding or not?" You can't always accurately pick up on the intended meaning. And stay away from sexual

Limit Texting and other Distractions During the Leg-Sniffing Phase.

messages, at least until your relationship is firmly established.)

- Failure to answer texts, emails and phone calls (Many times a person will say their phone fell into the toilet or they didn't get your text or email when they don't want to respond. Women are especially guilty of this. It's a snub. Watch out. I call it Selective Text and Voice Options, STVO.)
- Habitual lateness

Other Hazards

Like everything else, relationships are full of trade-offs. People will often settle for less satisfying sex, for example, if the person meets all of their other needs. Just make sure you're "settling" areas do not involve things that are really important to you.

I don't go for the "we were meant to be together" or "we're perfect" or "we're a 100 percent compatible match" mumbo jumbo. This is unrealistic hogwash. At the same time, don't just choose the pile of crap that stinks the least.

Be aware that when women insist on telling you certain things about themselves, it may be to compensate for a deficiency. For example, a woman might say she's really a nice person as a kind of decoy to throw you off when her nasty streak rears its ugly head. Or she may attempt to throw your horniness radar out of whack by saying she loves sex when she really doesn't like it very much. Talk about confusing a pig.

Beware of Choosing the Pile of Crap that Stinks the Least.

Rug Rats and Other Species of Kiddo

Okay. I admit it. I'm selfish. I've already raised kids and I'm not interested in sharing my love interest with her kids. I don't go for the widely acclaimed "it's all about the children" mindset. Look at the disastrous sense of entitlement that kind of thinking has bred. So before you dismiss me as a jerk pig, consider that reprioritizing the kids thing might save your relationship. And save the kids too.

Once you grow beyond the 25 to 35 year-old age bracket, it's pretty difficult to find someone who doesn't have kids. And kids are a big, big deal. They complicate the dating phase and beyond. That's why it's a good idea to go extra slow when kids are in the mix. It's next to impossible to develop a successful relationship when everything—from conversations to scheduling—is always about the kids.

Through my interviews as well as personal experience, I've discovered that women are more willing to accept kids than men are. No surprise there. Yet many women are wary of them too. And for good reason. Parents often aren't as accountable for their kids in new relationships as they should be. They don't intervene when their child is inconsiderate of the wishes and preferences of the new partner.

Worse, the parent often expects the new partner to shut up and take it. And a heap of crap crashes upon the new partner's head if he or she reprimands the new child. This breeds resentment and grinds down the primary relationship.

That's why I firmly believe that partners in new relationships should take priority over kids. After all, your very first romantic bond came before any child. You were number one to each other from the start. When you have children, you should still be number one to each other. It's actually better for all involved when the spouses' commitment to each other is the center of the family.

When you divorce and then enter into a new serious relationship or remarry, that priority should never change. You should always be willing to make the new partner or spouse number one, just as the old spouse was. If you can't do that, it's going to be a problem. The primary relationship will always suffer if it automatically takes a back seat to the kids. It does neither kids nor romantic bonds any good when kids are treated as if they're the center of the universe. It blows my mind that this isn't the mother of all "duhs."

Yeah, I know it's asking a lot. Blood is thicker than water. Parents use kids from prior relationships as weapons, excuses, and diversions. In many cases, we know our kids are rotten or whatever. But we don't want someone else to remind us of that.

One of my best friends says that it takes at least two years to get to know someone. I believe it. And I'll add that you don't *really* know them until you've done the laundry together, or taken out the trash, made the bed, and done all of the other life stuff that has to take place before we truly know someone.

My friend offers this advice: "Is there anything about them that bothers you, even a little? Make sure you know it and consider it. Because as you stay together longer and longer, those little things get much bigger and more annoying. And that pile can get huge and create a lot of negative energy."

CHAPTER 3

Pretty Girl Syndrome
(Pray it isn't contagious)

"The true man wants two things: danger and play. For that reason he wants woman, as the most dangerous plaything."
— Philosopher Friedrich Nietzsche

There's a saying that a beautiful woman is the most dangerous creature stalking the social scene. Women with boatloads of pretty wield a lot of power over men. And if you find yourself stuck in their orbit, it can get pretty ugly.

I coined the term Pretty Girl Syndrome (PGS) to describe the behaviors these women often let loose during the mating game. PGS is a disorder that hits women (and men, too—PBS) blessed with a bumper crop of beauty. Many attractive women suffer from PGS.

Now I'm not saying there aren't loving, unselfish and emotionally stable women out there who also happen to

Dabbling in the World of Pretty Girl Syndrome can be
Like Tip Toeing Through Alligators.

be beautiful. There are certainly more than a few. But, as a general rule, the more beautiful a woman is, the more likely she is to be an inconsiderate, self-absorbed head case.

Women with PGS have this loop constantly running through their heads: "I'm so pretty; I don't have to please you. Sure, I pretend to be sweet, unselfish, innocent, and accommodating. But when the rubber meets the road, I'm going to do what I want to do, when I want to do it."

Personally, I've always believed I could never meet and form romantic relationships with gorgeous women, though there have been exceptions. I operated under the assumption that a beautiful woman would snub me. So I didn't even try. Ultimately, I lost out. But so did she.

A beautiful woman usually won't hang on to a really good guy because of her vanity. When you spot a couple, where the girl on the guy's arm is more attractive than he is, you can bet he's a guy worth keeping (see Chapter 6). And she likely doesn't suffer from PGS. She is considerate. She is interested in pleasing her man.

But when a beautiful girl insists "oh he's got to be at least XX tall, and can't be over XXX pounds, and has to make $X,XXX,XXX per year," and she won't make any exceptions, she likely has a chronic case of PGS. She will struggle to hold on to a relationship with a *keeper,* even when she really wants to keep him. What she will have is a never-ending chain of broken relationships with not-so-great guys.

In *Power of the Pussy,* writer Kara King describes the typical conceited woman: she will only talk to "perfect" guys; she thinks she's prettier than most women; and she is quick to point out the flaws in other people as she pretends to be perfect.

King is describing pretty girl syndrome! In truth the PGS girl is a narcissist, pure and simple. It's all about her. And she's not above using sex as a weapon.

Most relationships with women with PGS are short—four months or so. Why? Because women with PGS are constantly checking the horizon for the more perfect guy. These women will keep dancing in and out of relationships until they find the man they feel is good enough for their beauty. What does a relationship with a woman suffering from PGS look like?

Meet Glenn and Cara

Glenn (not his real name) is a fit, recently divorced 40-something software entrepreneur. Glenn has enjoyed lots of business success. He rewards his hard work by wheeling around in an Aston Martin Vanquish. He met Cara, a media consultant in her mid-30s, at a bar that's become a hot spot for power players. With shoulder length brown hair, a drop-dead body, and a dimpled smile, Cara is striking. She has acres of charisma. She and Glenn hit it off immediately.

On the first date, Cara was dressed to kill. Her short skirt and spiky heels were flirty but classy. She laughed a lot and got a thrill talking about her work coaching executives on how to be sharp on camera. She didn't ask Glenn much about what he did, but that was okay because she was so entertaining. Still he thought it was odd when she asked him to describe the most expensive gift he had ever given a girl.

On the second date, the sexiness of her clothes went up a couple of notches. Her skirt was just a little tighter, her top had a deeper plunge, and her shoes were just a little spikier. The charm was still high-wattage, but when she asked him about his business, she seemed bored with his replies. It was as if she were waiting for him to finish so she could drop another name or point out another one of her professional conquests.

As they continued to date, Glenn noticed she grew more and more distracted whenever they were together. She answered every phone call and text. He also noticed she was rude to wait staff. At dinner, she would blow a gasket over the tiniest imperfections in her order and would routinely send food and drinks back. (On dates, there's also what I call "tomato syndrome." Some of the men I interviewed told me PGS girls would routinely say things like "Cut my tomatoes," or "I don't like lettuce," or "I hate black olives," yada yada yada—the battle cries of high maintenance girls.)

She also showed other suspicious behaviors. Wherever they went men would flirt with her. She loved the attention. Sometimes she would just smile and look away. But most of the time she egged them on. That these teases made Glenn uncomfortable seemed to give her a thrill.

While Cara seemed to project lots of sexual energy, Glenn discovered that she rarely wanted to get it on. She would tease and show interest only to withdraw at the last minute. "I have to get up early for a meeting tomorrow," she would say. After a couple of months, Glenn realized he was "getting it more like an old married guy." He always had to initiate.

When Glenn asked her about it, she accused him of having unreasonable expectations. She said that he set himself up for disappointment by assuming he'd get sex. It seemed to him she was avoiding sex because she really didn't like it, at least not with him. She couldn't relate to his sexual cravings, and didn't seem to care about them.

The Laugh that Means No

Several men I interviewed told me that when they expressed a desire to have sex with a beautiful woman they were dating, rather than give a yes or no answer, she would laugh seductively. She would lead him on, saying something like "that would be a cool place to have sex." But it would never seem to happen. These men said that at first they didn't really notice it. But they soon realized that when they suggested sex (and other activities) and she laughed, she really meant "no," or at a minimum was dodging the question. Women aren't above being tricky. Some back-out of sexual encounters while seeming to agree to them.

She would tease, flirt, promise—even cry when he told her that her lack of attention was hurtful—but never deliver.

While Cara insisted she loved spending time with Glenn, she increasingly became unavailable. She would cancel plans at the last minute because "something's come up" or "I have a conflict I forgot about." These conflicts always seemed to pop up on weekends.

Cara also seemed to have a "selective text and voice option (STVO)" on her phone and she responded to his calls and messages less frequently. "Your text didn't come through," she would say, or "I left my phone out in my car" or "I didn't get your call," or "my phone was dead."

She promised to call at appointed times and then didn't follow through.

Glenn soon saw a pattern. She would call or text only when she needed something, when it was convenient, or after he had gotten upset over her standoffishness.

Cara seemed honest at first. But Glenn noticed she had a habit of fibbing—especially when he asked about her whereabouts. When he confronted her about her ever-changing story lines, she would get pissy. Then she would cry. She would follow with promises to make it up to him. "I'll do better next time," she would say.

Glenn gave her the benefit of the doubt. He kept giving. He kept trying, believing she would be true to her word. But after weeks and months went by with no change, he called it quits.

The Fizzle of PGS Sizzle

With hindsight, Glenn realized what he was wrestling with, though he was blind to Cara's PGS symptoms while in the thick of the relationship. Cara couldn't change. PGS was simply too powerful. He viewed his months with Cara as a lot of wasted time. He grew cynical about women— especially pretty ones.

The guys I interviewed admitted they found it tough to connect with pretty women. Their beauty is intimidating. It's hard to meet them and even harder to turn that meeting into something more.

No wonder. Women with classic PGS don't know how to treat a man, and won't or can't keep a good one. But in her mind these faults don't matter because she's got so many guys chasing her. She thinks: I don't have to please you. I'm pretty. I'll just get a better date next Thursday.

The typical PGS girl gives just enough to keep her current guy interested until she gets bored. She will accommodate a man only when it is convenient for her or when she suspects he's at the end of his rope.

Just about every man I spoke with who had dated a really beautiful woman said the relationship was short-lived. And how could it not be? A woman with PGS will go through dozens of guys until all but the most beautiful, well-heeled ones have been dumped on the shoulder of the road. This isn't one-sided. Beautiful men (PBS) behave the same way, ditching all but the most beautiful women. And when you mix a PGS with a PBS you get a whole different thing altogether. Nitro.

Origins of PGS

What causes PGS? Here are my theories. PGS begins at an early age when boys begin favoring the prettiest girls. Maybe they had shapely bodies. Maybe they developed large breasts early. Whatever the reason, the boys chased after them. They sucked up to them.

When most girls were learning how to get the attention of boys (and appreciate themselves) with an eye on landing a balanced relationship, pretty girls bypassed these teachable moments. They never had to earn adoration. They knew they could get attention and dates anytime—anywhere—they wanted. Other girls were jealous of them. PGS girls got off on this. They learned to act as if they "didn't know" they were pretty, rubbing false modesty in everyone's face.

Their lack of curiosity means these girls probably never explored their bodies to any great extent. They didn't need to get in touch with themselves, or were raised to think sex was dirty or wrong. That's why they don't have much interest in sexually pleasing a man.

Research backs this up. According to *The Narcissist Epidemic: Living in the Age of Entitlement* by university psychologists Jean Twenge and W. Keith Campbell, narcissistic personality disorder (NPD) has been growing like algae blooms in a pig crap lagoon since 1980.

Much of the growth in NPD is among women. NPD-infected women tend to be overly emotional, obsess over their looks, itch for adoration, and have little self-awareness. They feel entitled to rewards without earning them. They are highly materialistic and have little interest in the give-and-take that makes for good relationships.

The authors blame the sharp rise in NPD on the growing obsession with celebrity and the self-esteem movement that was trendy in the 1970s and 80s. Kids got lots of praise, trophies just for showing up, and were given almost no incentive to develop strong character traits. Grade inflation was, and is, rampant ("A" is the new "C").

Parents wanted to be friends with their kids instead of being, you know, parents. They put themselves on an equal footing with their kids, thinking that this made them enlightened parents or something. Girls who in the past would have been disciplined for being spoiled brats were now telling their parents what's what. After decades of rewarding these bad behaviors, we're now harvesting a bumper crop of Pretty Girl Syndrome.

Women with full-blown PGS think they are so beautiful that everything in life will just fall into place in their favor. Their beauty will overcome any and all bad behaviors and outcomes. But what the PGS girl doesn't seem to realize is that "pretty" gets old—literally as well as figuratively.

They also seem unaware that sex with a pretty girl is pretty much the same as it is with a woman who is less foxy. Their looks might get a man's Willie to stand at attention more easily, but the flight through the goal posts is pretty much the same. Most men eventually realize the measly benefits don't justify the steep costs.

And when you get right down to it, beyond that initial stiffy, who actually gets turned on by a self-absorbed hellcat in heels anyway?

You May Have Scored a PGS Girl when she is:
- Unusually pretty
- Demanding of constant praise and adoration
- Standoffish and noncommittal
- Almost never apologetic or accepting of responsibility
- Prone to deflect accountability by throwing it back on you
- Likely to think her problems outweigh yours, no matter how small—even tiny things have drama

- Overly confident in her appearance (though she may also be coy about her beauty and appearance)
- Prone to envy
- Infuriated when inconvenienced
- Unpredictable
- Lacking in empathy (especially for your sexual needs)
- Prone to blame others for her problems
- Inclined to overdo apologies if backed into a corner, but quickly resumes the offending behaviors. She can talk a good game, fake remorse, etc., but can't walk the talk
- Dishonest and lies to get what she wants, though she appears very honest (she may be very honest in matters that *don't* benefit her)
- Unlikely to show any genuine interest in you or your passions
- Rude to those she sees as beneath her
- Curious about how much money you have
- Secretive about where she is and what she's been up to
- Very sexual at first, but quickly turns icy
- Unwilling to initiate sex or engage in sexually adventurous activity
- Prone to use sex as a weapon to manipulate and keep you off balance
- Skilled at fishing for compliments
- Non-committal about her availability (she's waiting for a better offer)
- Quick with excuses when she falls short of your expectations, but promises to do better

- Unlikely to invest any effort to accommodate your needs and desires
- Loaded to the gills with deal breakers and filters for evaluating who she will date, and who she will dump
- Flirty with lots of guys, keeping them interested while holding them at bay
- Equipped with STVO on her cell phone

CHAPTER 4

Sex, Sex, Sex
The Elephant in the Room. Time to Talk

"Sex alleviates tension. Love causes it."
— WOODY ALLEN

"There's very little advice in men's magazines, because men don't think there's a lot they don't know. Women do. Women want to learn. Men think, 'I know what I'm doing. Just show me somebody naked.'"
— JERRY SEINFELD

"You know why God is a man? Because if God was a woman she would have made sperm taste like chocolate."
— COMEDIENNE CARRIE SNOW

During my research and interviews with both men and women, I began to notice a funny thing. All of the men I spoke with who were in a long-term relationship (with the exception of two lucky guys) said they weren't getting enough sex. All of the women I interviewed said—without fail—that they loved sex. Some 30 percent of these women even said they wanted *more* sex.

So: All of the men aren't getting enough sex. All of the women said they love sex and some wish they could get more sex. What is wrong with this picture?

There's more. Most of the women said they were getting enough sex, but they didn't seem aware (or care?) that their men wanted more sex. They thought their men were getting enough, thank you very much. And while the men were telling *me* they weren't getting enough sex, they weren't telling their wives or girlfriends they weren't getting enough sex. So they drag their feet through their relationships unsatisfied. Or they cheat.

That's one huge elephant in the room. It's a big unspoken disconnect between expectations and reality. If the vast majority of men want more sex at the same time their women think these same men are getting plenty of sex and at least a few of these women wish *they* could get more sex, that's not a simple case of miscommunication. That's a communications disaster. (It's also a lot of "sex" packed into two paragraphs, but that's not important right now).

People aren't talking. I don't think that surprises anybody though.

Men and Sex: What Women Don't Get

For the most part, women don't want to have sex with a man if they don't have an emotional attachment—or at least a physical attraction—to him. Also: Women generally don't want to have sex when they feel unattractive.

The same isn't true for most men. Men don't need an emotional or a physical attraction. And if they look good because they've showered, shaved, and brushed their teeth, that's great. But these grooming exercises certainly aren't a priority. The truth is these things take a back seat. Men just want to get laid.

And getting laid is hardwired into men. According to "Sexual Exploitability: Observable Cues and Their Link to Sexual Attraction," an article published in *Evolution and Human Behavior* (Summer 2012), men and women use different benchmarks to decide when to have sex.

Men are programmed to look for easy sex. They don't care much about the consequences. Women are instinctively gun-shy. They're born with a brain that makes them highly aware of the consequences of casual sex.

No surprise here. We forget that up until about 100 years ago, before things like antibiotics, labor-inducing drugs, and commonplace surgeries, pregnancy was a risky business. And this was true socially and economically (out of wedlock births) as well as physically. In those days, death rates for women and infants during childbirth were high. Between 1900 and 1997, deaths in childbirth plummeted by 99 percent for mothers and more than 90 percent for infants, according to the Centers for Disease Control.

In terms of biology, sperm is cheap and plentiful. Men produce something like 85 million sperm cells per testicle per day. For women, eggs are expensive and in short supply.

That's why for our female ancestors having lots of sex partners wouldn't do much for their reproductive success and could actually harm it.

Men, on the other hand, increase the survivability of their "oats" by sowing them far and wide. Men instinctively look for the low-hanging fruit. They scan for telltale cues from women to see if they're easy. These can be things like a "come hither" look, revealing dress, recklessness, immaturity, intoxication, a slow wit, and gullibility.

Yet these same traits make women less desirable to men as long-term mates. I mean a woman who comes off as easy makes her a potential conquest for other men. What guy wants that?

There's more. For a man, sex solves a lot of problems. It releases endorphins. It unleashes positive energy. A man's whole makeup is sex-centric. Physically something happens. Emotionally a man is renewed after he has sex.

Sexual energy and that quest to sow oats drive almost everything he does. It's the source of his creativity (do you think there would be a Picasso, The Beatles' *Sergeant Pepper's Lonely Hearts Club Band*, or an Empire State Building without the male focus on sex?). So he has to go back to the well every now and again for a fill-up. Some men get worse mileage than others.

For men, the costs of not having sex are often greater than the benefits of having sex. As the saying goes: *Losing hurts more than winning feels good.*

If I go more than 3 days without sex, I get irritable. I did find some men who said they don't care that much

Keeping the Spark Hot

Differing expectations about sex is one of the biggest sources of relationship strife. So says the *Wall Street Journal* ("How Often Should Married Couples Have Sex?" April 22, 2013). Experts believe sex is a more emotional experience for men than it is for women. Men tend to express their feelings with actions, not words. They relate to their partner through sex, and for many it is their primary mode of communication. So what happens when the man wants sex and he doesn't get it? His primary emotional outlet gets kicked to the curb. He gets resentful and cranky. He puts on weight. He checks out. He cheats.

What to do? According to a study in the May 2013 issue of *Social Psychological and Personality Science*, people are better able to keep the flame hot and flickering when they are motivated to meet their partner's sexual needs—even when these needs conflict with their own preferences. They're willing to get it on even when it doesn't necessarily turn *them* on. The key: They expect their partner will do the same for them, but it isn't an immediate quid pro quo.

about sex. I am not sure if they just don't know what they don't know, or they are just wound a little differently. But they're out there. And they are a good fit for women with similar preferences.

Sex is how a man connects with the world. When a woman *wants* to please her man sexually—actually initiates sex every once in a while—a man feels desired and loved. It's not the cooking. It's not washing and folding his boxers. It's not bringing him an unsolicited beer while he's vegging in front of the big screen. It's sex, sex, sex!

Now that may sound piggish. And it is. After all, it doesn't work the other way around.

But face it. It's the truth. If a woman doesn't seem genuinely interested in pleasing her man physically, or if she acts like it's a bother, deep down he doesn't think she's that into him. He resents it. Then he gets angry (some of the men I interviewed were genuinely pissed off). Then he shuts down.

Most men won't admit to this. They'd rather die. They don't want to be mocked as a pig or accused of being selfish (even though both parties benefit from sex—*the big disconnect*). They don't want to be put into a position where they have to beg. So they clam up. Enter communications breakdown. And maybe an extra girlfriend, which I personally don't advocate.

Low Libido Men?

Yet, are some women just as sexually neglected as many men? Yes says clinical social worker Michele Weiner Davis. Davis, author of the bestseller *The Sex-Starved Wife: What to Do When He's Lost Desire*, says that while more men than women complain about not getting enough sex, the difference between guys and gals is not as great as we're led to believe. "Low desire in men has got to be America's best-kept secret," she says in an interview published April 7, 2008 in *Time* magazine.

Davis collaborated with *Redbook* magazine to survey women about their sex lives. A whopping 60 percent of the more than 1,000 women who responded reported that they wanted as much—if not more—sex than their boyfriends or husbands. The vast majority of their men were completely unwilling to talk about their lack of interest in sex or see a doctor or a therapist to remedy the problem. These guys are tight-lipped, Davis says, because we live in a culture that equates manliness with turbo-charged sex drives.

There are lots of reasons for low desire in men, says Davis. For example, most antidepressants and medications for cardiovascular disease can wilt a man's Willie. Ditto the low testosterone levels that often come with age (see "Macho Menopause," Chapter 8). To these, you can add relationship issues such as critical or nagging mates who often clam men up and drive them into a cave.

But there are other issues too. Davis admits she gets tons of e-mails from men who say they've lost interest because their women have totally let themselves go. They don't eat well. They don't exercise. They walk around all day in sweatpants. Their women don't chase after them. It makes a man feel as though his wife or girlfriend doesn't think he or the relationship is worth the trouble. So his attraction to her drains away.

Now many women may think this is just plain piggish and shallow. Yet for men physical attraction is a very basic, animalistic thing. Arousal in men is more oriented towards the visual—that wiring thing again. If these women really want their mates to be more sexually interested in them, they should pay more attention to their appearance and not take it for granted (see "How'd I End up with 40 Miles of Rough Road?" in Chapter 7).

Men really are very simple. And for women this is a good thing. There's no second-guessing a man. There's no need to try and read his mind. You *know* what's on his mind. Sex is the most cost-effective way for a woman to take care of her man and reap the rewards of a better relationship. There's no better bang for the buck than banging the buck. Every man's fantasy is a lady in the streets and a freak in the sheets. So my advice to women: FREAK OUT already.

Of Mice and Men

Maybe you need more convincing that men and women have different brains—that their wiring is different. So let's bring in the scientists.

Researchers from the University of Alberta (*Science Daily*, 2005) let a group of male and female volunteers loose in a big maze. They asked them to get through the maze and make their way back to the starting point as quickly as possible. The result? On average, the men made their way back to the starting point more than three times faster than the women.

But the women were able to recall the features of the route in greater detail. For the men, the entire trip was a blur. They focused single-mindedly on the goal: finding their way back as quickly as possible. The women took a more "holistic" approach to the task. This difference may explain why women want romance and foreplay and men want to get laid.

Researchers at the University of Pittsburgh (*Journal of Comparative Psychology*, March 1990) tested this maze puzzle with voles, which are mouse-like burrowing rodents. They did it with two kinds of voles: the meadow vole and the prairie vole. Male meadow voles are promiscuous "pigs" that roam far and wide in search of food and sex. Prairie voles are monogamous homebodies.

After putting the voles through the maze trick, the researchers discovered that the hornier meadow voles figured out the maze in no time flat. The prairie voles took much longer, as did the female voles of both species.

They discovered another interesting thing. After dissecting the vole's brains, they found that an area called the hippocampus was much bigger in the sex-crazed meadow voles than it was in either the male prairie vole or the female voles. The hippocampus is thought to help humans form mental maps and navigate unfamiliar places.

Some biologists think that our male human ancestors were like those horny meadow voles. To survive and thrive, they roamed great distances endlessly chasing game and girls. The upshot is they became highly skilled at forming mental maps and getting their bearings in strange surroundings (now you know why men don't ask for directions—*they never get lost*—oink!). Females and homebody males? Not so much. Making a home takes a different skillset.

This is why men seem so single-minded about tasks, goals, "getting to the point," and . . . *sex*. Think of it this way: if men weren't pigs, humans might not have survived long enough to invent remote-controlled sex toys. And what a bummer that would be.

Why Most Women Don't Like Sex (as much)

Overall, women don't focus on sex nearly as much as men do. Need proof? Hell no. But let's bring in the scientists again anyway.

According to one study (*The Social Organization of Sexuality: Sexual Practices in the United States*, Laumann, Gagnon, Michael, Michaels, 1994), 54 percent of men think about sex at least once every day. That compares to just 19 percent of women who think such thoughts daily. That's one elephant-sized gap.

But here's the interesting thing. According to a national survey (*National Survey of Sexual Health and Behavior* 2010, www.nationalsexstudy.indiana.edu), more women than men reported having sex in the past year, at least among younger people (18-29). Yet when you get past age 30, those numbers reverse. Big time. Between the ages of 30 and 69, more men than women reported having sex in the last year. The biggest gaps are between 30 and 39 (men 85 percent, women 74 percent), and 60 and 69 (men 54 percent, women 42 percent).

So what does this mean? Hell if I know. What I've discovered in my interviews is that about 20 percent of women are crazy about sex. Another 20 percent don't like sex at all, although that doesn't necessarily mean they're asexual. The remaining 60 percent is somewhere in between, with most in the middle.

What's important is that those women in that top 20 percent *need* sex. They're like most men. They get irritable when they don't get it. That 20-percent girl is the Holy Grail (see Chapter 5). These women also like crazy sex. Crazy sex is whatever you define it to be. To some people, it's making love with the lights on. For others, it's strap-ons, swinging (either in lifestyles or from the ceiling), leather and handcuffs, or an orgy.

But mostly it's about being insatiable. The top 20-percent girl just can't get enough. When a man is in a committed relationship, it's very appealing to be with a woman who wants a lot of sex. Maybe it's my imagination, but the women in this group seemed to project more positive energy. The men who were with a "twenty-percenter" were, of course, very happy indeed. And it showed.

Then again, there are actually some men who don't like the top 20-percent girl. These men want to be totally dominating, always in charge. They don't want to be chased—and maybe dominated—by a woman with a libido as big and powerful as a Mack truck. They want to chase her. They want to be the source of everything sexual for her.

Still the question remains: why is it that most women seem to have less interest in sex than men do? Some of the women I interviewed said they're simply old-fashioned or that they don't want to be pegged as sluts. These are the reasons that they don't pursue a man, initiate sex, or show an interest in frequent sex.

But I think these women are just being selfish. Any woman who likes lots of sex and loves to please the man she is committed to is not a slut. Enjoying sex in a committed relationship is not slutty.

One man I interviewed told me his girlfriend complained that men have set their expectations too high. A man can't just automatically expect sex after every nice dinner or special occasion, she said. Women want it to be more spontaneous, a surprise moment.

I heard a number of other complaints from women. Men refuse to do what turns their women on—sexually or otherwise—they say. Men cum too fast. Men pay little—if any—attention to foreplay. Lots of women told me that men don't like to provide oral sex. (One man said his woman loved getting oral sex but refused it because she was raised to think it was dirty.)

But on average the stats don't back up many of these complaints (NSSHB 2010). Sure, more women give oral sex to men than the other way around between the ages of 18 and 29. But once you get past the age of 30, men take over. For example, between the ages of 30 and 39, 59 percent of women gave oral sex to men. But that compares to 69 percent of men who gave oral sex to women. Women close the gap slightly between 40 and 59. But the gap grows again between 60 and 69: 34 percent of men are givers compared to just 23 percent of women.

It doesn't take much for a man to get off. For women, it's more complicated. Many women say their most satisfying relationship experiences come from just being connected. They don't base satisfaction just on orgasms. Yet women are far more likely to get off when sexual activity includes oral sex as well as nooky. It's likely just an expectations gap that can be overcome by being aware of the differences in our brains.

The Power of Finishing A Head

It's called BJTC, and it's a beautiful if scarce thing. In less polite terms, it's known as Blow Jobs To Completion. And it's a conundrum.

Most women will give a man oral sex at one time or another. But they generally stop just short of the hallelu-jah chorus. This is extremely frustrating for most guys. It's like quail hunting with a popgun. Or drag racing on a Segway.

Based on what I learned from my interviews, few women enjoy giving a man oral sex. Even fewer enjoy BJTC, or fellatio to finale, or whatever you want to call it.

By my estimate, at most, one in four women will per-form oral sex to its proper conclusion. The sad part? Many women willingly perform BJTC in the early stages of a relationship. They do them as part of the wooing process. But once they're secure in the relationship, they drop them.

Maybe they believe they've paid their dues and they're just "done with that."

Why is this? They focus on the act instead of on pleasing their mate. They fixate on the alleged unpleasantness of BJTC instead of on the pleasure it brings to their man. Some women say they don't like the taste of semen or the feel or whatever. But we're disgusted by the taste of Nyquil too. But we take it because it helps us sleep.

Still, I found several women who love giving BJTC. They gave many reasons, but mostly they said it makes them feel in control; it gives them a sense of power. They also know it makes them a highly appreciated mate.

The fact is if a woman is willing to perform BJTC as part of the courtship process, it's just selfish to quit once the relationship is nailed down. It's like these women believe it's no longer necessary to please their man, and they can get away with it.

Most men will resent this deeply, even if they don't admit it. This resentment will come out in other ways. This is especially true if the man is willing to do whatever he can to please his woman and the favor isn't returned.

A lot of women have a hard time understanding why men want blowjobs. They chalk it up to the fact that they're pigs and getting off is all they care about. Men can just lay back and get off without having to lift a finger (no different from when a man gives a woman oral sex, by the way).

But the truth is men love oral sex because it is one of the most powerful ways a woman can show she loves and admires her man. She's willing to be vulnerable to him.

She's as connected to the heart of his manhood as she can be, and it shows she won't reject that manhood. This is a powerful statement for a man.

My advice: do whatever you can to reach a compromise. For most men, BJTC is very important. He will take it as a strong sign of affection from a woman who offers it willingly. Women, if you agree to do it, don't act like it's an unpleasant obligation. Most men would rather you not bother.

Note: I did find some women who said their man wouldn't allow them to finish (though I didn't find any men who would admit this).

The Big Disconnect: Internet Porn

Internet porn has exploded with the advent of everywhere, always on digital connectivity. This isn't a good thing. I think Internet porn is dangerous (I'm making a distinction here between readily available Internet porn and conventional porn like DVDs). It's easy to become obsessed with the stuff, and I don't think that's healthy. In the long run, it's likely driving a wedge between men and women, deadening relationships.

There have been a few articles over the last few years on how the porn onslaught may be gradually changing the male libido. Porn's easy availability is making men immune to the charms of real women. One sex counselor coined the phenomenon "sexual attention deficit disorder."

In *Playboy* (February 2010), John Mayer called Internet porn a new "synaptic pathway," meaning I guess it changes a man's brain wiring. "You wake up in the morning, open a thumbnail page, and it leads to a Pandora's box of visuals," says the 34-year-old singer-songwriter. "There have probably been days when I saw 300 [naked girls] before I got out of bed . . . Internet pornography has absolutely changed my generation's expectations. . . . How does that [porn] not affect the psychology of having a relationship with somebody? It's got to."

Real women must seem like aliens to men who spend a lot of time getting turned on by porn stars in high definition. If stimulation only comes from overstimulation, a typical woman doesn't stack up. She isn't porn-worthy.

Internet porn is okay if the both of you are comfortable with it. But if porn images and scenarios become the ideal that real sex is measured against, you need to rethink your Internet porn habit. Being too big an Internet porn hound may even deaden your ability to relate to a flesh-and-blood sex partner—*Stunted Arousal Syndrome*.

Still, a little porn here and there can be stimulating. So I am not going to throw the baby out with the bath water. Or the piglet out with the slop bucket.

CHAPTER 5

The Holy Grail

27 Traits That Indicate Your Girl *Really* Needs Sex

"Man is the only creature who has a nasty mind."
— MARK TWAIN

Remember that girl who blew your mind with her sexual appetite and daring? You may have met her in a bar, at a party, in the grocery store, or at the dentist's office. Or maybe you met her on that flight home for Thanksgiving.

Anyway, it wasn't long before you were back at her place. As soon as you walked through the door she was peeling off her clothes. (No need for her to slip off her panties. She wasn't wearing any.) Next thing you knew she was spread out on the floor hand-cuffed to a case of Reddi-Wip.

She proceeded to screw your lights out. She quickly flipped them back on, only to screw them out again. Change blown fuses. Disinfect wounds. Rub in Bengay. Rinse. Repeat.

These are women with turbo-charged sexual energy. They have a certain presence; a damn-the-torpedoes horniness that drives them to try anything, anywhere, anytime. Or is it all the time?

Just about every man I interviewed had experienced a girl like this at one point in his life. A lot of these encounters occurred while the men I interviewed were in college with women of a similar age. Other men met their sexual tigress when both were in their 40s or even older. Regardless of when they crossed paths, men remember these insatiable women. Fondly. Longingly.

Among the 40 to 50-year-old women with voracious sexual appetites, is it just that they somehow discovered the secret to keeping a man happy (not with the cooking)? Or did they just grow comfortable with their bodies— even when imperfect—and sexuality as they entered the prime of their lives, with the stresses of kids and prior soured relationships a distant memory? I didn't solve that mystery.

So who are these women? Alas, they make up no more than 20 percent of the lady pool. Tops. Many of the girls these men remember so fondly may not even be a part of the 20 percent. They might have just been going through a short crazy-sex phase in their youth.

The challenge is finding the ones who were not in a phase, but were blessed with the crazy-sex gene. That's what this chapter will help men do. Of course, there's the additional challenge of finding a woman with the crazy-sex gene who isn't also psycho; one who is stable and meets your other requirements. And visa versa.

These men described in detail the traits and behaviors these women had. I compiled a list of the ones I heard

Be Careful What You Wish for: The Girl with the Crazy Sex Gene can also be a Little Psycho.

the most often. Just to be clear: this list doesn't describe women who *love* sex. It describes women who *need* sex. Many women *say* they love sex and want sex. But few really need it.

Another thing: These women are not sluts, looking to fill some other need with sex. Their need for sex is primal; it's part of who they are.

About the list and the interviews. It's funny really. People will tell you almost *anything* if you ask. And asking the questions the right way can bring up insights that surprise even the interviewee. I challenged men to tell me about *that girl*, the one who was different from all of the others.

Key questions: "What was it about her that set her apart? What characteristic was unique to her?" They would smile, shake their head and say something like: "Oh, yea, I remember her. She was one of a kind. What made her different? She *always* wanted to watch porn."

Use this list as a field guide to pick these women out from the crowd. Then do your best to woo them into your orbit.

Of course, no one woman exhibits all of these traits. Most highly sexed women will have just three or four. A woman with more than a few may indicate a sexually explosive personality. Beware. The list is not in any particular order.

- **Wholesome Cravings.** Sees sex as a good thing, hungers for it, and knows how to feed that hunger.

A Word about the Holy Grail Discovery

I stumbled on the Holy Grail by asking two questions. The third person I interviewed for this book told a vivid story about a prior girlfriend who was a beast in the sack because she "needed sex." After that interview, I started to ask men if they remembered a girl who had an unusual sexual appetite—who seemed to need sex. Virtually all could remember at least one. I followed up by asking, "Can you recall anything that was different about that girl?"

That was the trigger. They would pause, their eyes would light up and they would say something like, "Oh, Yea, Her. She carried a vibrator in her purse. I never dated another girl who did that." The Holy Grail was the result of this questioning. Every item on this list was mentioned by at least one interviewee, most by more than one.

- **No Panties.** She doesn't wear panties. She likes it that way. She flashes you. Going panty-less makes her feel sexy.
- **Stockings.** She routinely wears thigh highs and stockings with garter belts. Bonus points for fishnets. Note: younger women may not get the stockings and garter belt thing. Think of this as a teachable moment.

- **Adult Stores.** She asks to be taken to adult stores to shop for toys, garments, videos and restraints. Or she goes herself. Better: she makes you go with her by using the restraints she just bought.
- **Remote control.** She makes frequent use of remote control vibrators and vibrating panties. She has a special place in her heart for the wireless kind.
- **Porn.** She wants to watch porn. She asks for porn. She even brings the DVDs. Remember: most women will watch porn; some require more wine than others.
- **Alarm cock.** She likes to wake you up with a good-morning blowjob.
- **Always Prepared.** She regularly needs orgasms. And she's always packing: she carries a vibrator in her purse. She's likely to use it at the office, in the mall, or in the car. Remember the first rule of defensive driving: watching out for on-coming drivers.
- **Topless Bars.** She asks to go to a topless or nude bar every once in a while. Or takes you there herself. Don't forget to put a few ten spots in the panties she isn't wearing.
- **Direct.** She's very direct about sex—even aggressive. She doesn't ask for sex. She demands it. She tells you she needs it. She tells you what you're going to do to fill that need. She will tell you to eat her kitty. *Meow.* Oops. I mean "oink."
- **Talks Dirty.** She never needs an excuse to (secretly) talk dirty to you. It's a second language to her. Her sweet

nothings are always just a little saucier, a little nastier. She'll whisper these nothings in your ear during dinner, a movie, a family gathering, a concert, a lecture, or a sermon. She'll double your fun if she knows sign language. In the bedroom, she gets a little louder.

- **Rubs.** She'll rub your wick under the table while at dinner with others. Or while you're driving. Or while negotiating a big purchase or business deal. Remember: Don't take your eye off the decimal point. This is more important than it might seem. Most men like to be chased. Just like a woman does. She knows this. Intuitively. She'll grab your ass while giving you a hug. She'll dole out a crotch grab while whispering in your ear she wants *that*. Of course, she's always discreet.

- **Adventurous.** She asks to experiment, insists on it. She always wants to try new positions, new toys, new flavors, and new lawns in the neighborhood. One of the guys said these special women have the "explorer" gene.

- **Photogenic.** She encourages and/or keeps sensual photos and videos of herself. She may even ask you nicely to star in some of them. And she will *for sure* help you make a good movie.

- **BJTC.** She loves this. You won't have to ask. And she actually wants you to finish (she wouldn't have it any other way). It makes her feel SO powerful, having that much control over you.

- **Loves Oral Sex.** Almost the same as the prior listing, except, well, she likes receiving. Don't be surprised if she jumps up and sits on your face.
- **Considerate.** She brings you the Viagra on a serving plate to let you know what she's thinking.
- **K.O.** She will have sex after a fight. A woman who needs sex still needs sex, even after the heat of battle. And it's not "make up" sex. It's "get on with it already" sex.
- **Clothing Optional.** She likes being naked anytime, all of the time; while vacuuming, doing laundry, preparing breakfast, or watching TV. It stimulates her, makes her feel sexy. Her comfort with her body gives her sexual confidence.
- **Public Sex.** She loves sex. Anywhere. She's not afraid to follow you into a public restroom, cluster under a bridge on the river walk, or proposition you at 31,000 feet. She's a risk taker, this girl.
- **Dress for Success.** She dresses sexy to please herself, though she hopes she will get lucky (pleasing you). She works at looking good. Many of the guys I interviewed wondered: Why is that once a girl turns 40 she cuts her hair and throws out her thongs and come-hither heels? Not this girl (unless you want that).
- **Deviant.** Not. She doesn't think a man is a pervert just because he wants lots of crazy sex. In fact, she admires him for it.
- **Initiative.** She will have sex almost anywhere (did I already say that?), any time, and in any manner. She

initiates sex. Regularly. She is always ready, willing, and hoping you are.

- **Inquiring Mind.** She has an innate curiosity about sex. She asks questions and loves to share what she's learned. She's a quick study too.
- **Handy.** She thinks there is an issue with the relationship if there isn't frequent sex. She'll look for solutions. She's eager to fix it.
- **Fantasies.** She fearlessly shares her sexual fantasies, and wants to hear yours. She figures out how to make all of them come true.
- **Sexual awareness at an early age.** I found a number of women who discovered that "wonderful feeling"—the orgasm—at ages as early as 8. Once they discovered that feeling, they were on a mission to experience it again and again, on into adulthood. They learned to really like sex early on, and need lots of it.

In her book *The Good Girl's Guide to Bad Girl Sex*, sex therapist Barbara Keesling, Ph.D., includes a "Being Bad" list that is similar to my Holy Grail list. It outlines why some girls are just better at—and presumably want more—sex than other girls.

For instance, Keesling says the typical girl who has a bad day at work and fights traffic on the way home will have little or no interest in sex when she finally gets there. But a good girl who likes "bad girl sex" builds anticipation and relieves stress by fantasizing about great sex on the way home instead of fixating on work and traffic. Guess what she wants when she walks through the door?

This book helps women rediscover everything *good* about being truly *bad*. It should be required reading.

Amusing Vignettes

As I've said, people will tell you the darndest things if you just ask them. I think people should get over the idea that asking people personal questions—and really listening to their answers—is nosey or rude. Most people appreciate it when you show a sincere interest in what they have to say. People are hungering to be heard (especially that sack mate you're neglecting).

Here a few amusing snippets I've collected while researching the Holy Grail:

The Naked Truth. One man I interviewed—63-years-old, married 40 years—gave me two for the list. I was excited to hear from someone married so long and wanted to know his and her secret. ONE: His wife loves being naked. No, it's not about making him horny. It's about making *herself* horny. She loves her body and her sexuality. TWO: She doesn't wait for him to take action. She brings him the Viagra. She decides when she *is* going to be satisfied. How refreshing!

Concealed Carry. One girl got downright offended (defensive?) when I introduced her to some of the items on the

Holy Grail list. The idea that a girl would actually carry a vibrator in her purse riled her. "That's crazy," she said. "Someone made that up." She went on to quiz her friend who worked for the Transportation Security Administration (TSA) and reported that her friend had never come across a vibrator in a purse. (No doubt many more carry them in their luggage.)

That doesn't mean it isn't so. During my interviews, I discovered two women who carried them in their purses. One claimed hers went off accidently while she was attending a funeral. Her friends thought her phone was ringing. But she had bumped it and turned it on.

Always On. In one interview, a younger woman told me that her desire for sex centered on the man: chemistry, how she felt about him, how he treated her, etc. These feelings and behaviors are big keys to female arousal, but they can just as easily be turned into excuses for not wanting sex. *"It's his fault."*

But make no mistake: the women possessing Holy Grail traits—the 20 percenters—won't use these excuses. They *need* sex, just like men do. Yes, sex is always better with someone you truly love, but they want and need sex in and of itself. (Men say they never have bad sex, it's just that some sex is better than other sex.) This is why a 20 percenter might carry a vibrator in her purse, for instance. She's simply not going to wait for the man to give her what she needs.

Use This List in a Positive Way

While this list isn't exhaustive, it's a damn good start. Ladies: don't fret. It was rare that the men I interviewed described a woman who possessed more than three or four of these traits. So don't feel compelled to start ticking them off to see if you measure up. Instead, consider the list a self-help guide. Pick a few items that you're comfortable with (and that would impress your man) and expand from there if it makes sense. Think of it as a way to improve your relationship. If you're lucky, your pig will respond favorably and even give you the pedestal treatment (see Chapter 10).

Remember, the Holy Grail describes a 20-percent girl, or one in five women. Many 20-percent girls are discrete and no doubt loathe the TSA (grope, grope). In addition, most 20-percent girls have just a few of these traits while others may have more. There is no standard. Being defensive isn't going to make it true or untrue, right or wrong.

Now some women may read this chapter or this list and feel that the women who have these traits are "sluts" or "whores" or "pigs". But it's simply not the case. These women are *ladies* with above average sex drives. It's unfortunate that this list incenses so many women and drives them to hurl insults.

I think the list riles some women because they feel they don't measure up to what many men are seeking. Because they can't or won't consider being like the 20-percent girl, they feel the need to insult her.

It's true that some people don't like, want, or need lots of sex, but they aren't likely to read this book. The rest of us who do like sex love 20-percent girls. Oink Oink.

Show Us Yours

The Holy Grail List is a work in progress. We're soliciting your ideas on which traits reveal those women who NEED sex. What have we missed? Post your suggestions to the Holy Grail list at MenArePigsBook.com. If we add your suggestions to the list, you can receive attribution plus five free copies of the next edition of *Men are Pigs*.

CHAPTER 6

What a Guy Worth Keeping Wants

"Every woman needs one man in her life who is strong and responsible. Given this security, she can proceed to do what she really wants to do: fall in love with men who are weak and irresponsible."
— CANADIAN HUMOR COLUMNIST RICHARD J. NEEDHAM

"The only thing worse than a man you can't control is a man you can."
— HUMORIST MARGO KAUFMAN

You're probably asking: who are these keeper guys?

Imagine if you will a ruthlessly efficient system for weeding out the trash fish (suckers, carp, river chubs) from the dating pool. A good system would allow you to zero in on the best prospects (trout, salmon, Bluefin tuna).

You could easily filter the "most eligible" candidates from the larger school of suckers and chubs. Think of the huge savings of time and money. Think of the savings in sanity.

Face it: most of the good men and women are taken. That doesn't mean they don't get circulated back into the pool though. The trick is to know how to bait your hook to snag the prize catches. Tip: Don't use dough balls and chicken gizzards if you want to land Chinook.

Most women agree that the best men have a steady job, an even-keeled personality, and a low-to-moderate thirst for alcohol. Plus they're organized, well groomed, and thoughtful. Maybe tender. Oh, and they know how to get a woman hyperventilating in bed.

The Ultimate Weeding System

 How do you tease the trout from the carp? My ideal system would start with a credit score checkup. Why credit scores? Because people who handle their business—*handle their business*. They cross their "t's," dot their "i's."

On the other hand, those who feel entitled tend to stiff people. They live beyond their means, emotionally as well as materially. They run up credit balances and expect their debts to be forgiven. They think they're owed. And they will have 101 reasons or excuses why it isn't their fault, why they've been mistreated and screwed.

Sometimes the Best Way to Separate the Winners from the Losers
is to Start with a Wallet Biopsy.

Now nearly everyone gets into financial trouble at least once during his or her lifetime. And while a credit score isn't a complete snapshot of a person, a low score is a useful warning of potential problems. If someone willingly sponges cash resources from others and feels little or no obligation to repay them, how likely is it that person will respect the emotional resources in a relationship?

Of course, this system for landing keepers is unrealistic. You can't check a potential mate's credit score without their permission (damn!).

But you can spot these risky creatures by tuning your radar to pick up certain habits and complaints. Are they resentful or envious? Do they think all banks, airlines, auto dealers, and insurance and oil companies are out to rip them off? Do they short change service staff? Do they feel justified swiping hotel towels, restaurant silver-ware, and far more than their share of department store samples and complimentary mints? Do they frequently have their credit cards rejected when settling the bill or making purchases?

To most women a good catch is a guy who is stable, has aspirations, and displays a sweet disposition. That's why the good guys have lots of women chasing them, right? Um, not so much.

And as I've stated before, so many women are making excuses for jerk boyfriends who are flakes and don't have any money. For some reason, they seem to think that it is in their best interest to be mommy to a man-child when they could be dating a much better man.

Women Don't Really Want What They Say They Want

Women tend to look at all the wrong guys in all the wrong places and think they're going to stumble upon, you know, *Mr. Right*. The typical woman will date a jerk followed by different jerk, topped off by yet another jerk until she finally hits upon a keeper. But after landing that keeper, more often than not, she won't treat him right. She'll dis him. She'll start looking for someone who is better looking with a better pedigree and a better job. The relationship ends and she goes right back to that string (or is it circle?) of jerks.

Why is this? Because most women really don't want "good guys" as they describe them. Instead, they want a guy who is dominant, who struts his stuff and shakes things up. Women want men who are more than a little cocky,

Women and Jerks?
Blame it on Hormones

 Why do so many women pursue men who are attractive and charming but unreliable, conniving jerks? According to a study from the University of Texas at San Antonio, women show a strong preference for charismatic, dominant cads when they're ovulating. Hormones released during ovulation drive them to favor sexy jerks, who will probably cheat on and dump them, over reliable, stable "nice" guys.

Published in *Journal of Personality and Social Psychology* (May 14, 2012), the study shows women often delude themselves into thinking sexy bad boys will magically turn into devoted husbands and top-notch dads. So when women moan about the shortage of nice guys, remind them that the makeup of the man pool is largely driven by female preferences. When it comes to reproductive success, nice "beta" guys really do finish last. To that, I'll add pigs are famous for producing big litters. So keep oinkin'.

alpha males who know how to comfortably take charge and get things done. In interview after interview women have told me they want a man with confidence (and many aren't afraid to add "in bed").

The guy these women really want is perfectly willing to spank their fanny every once in a while (playfully, of

Some Women Swear that Putting Lipstick on a Jerk Will Suddenly Turn them into Brad Pitt Pig.

course), especially in bed. Now the typical woman would rather die than admit this is the stuff of keepers. She may even find the idea offensive. Until she finds a man who does it. Trust me on this one.

Most true keepers are bad boys in one way or another. They're exciting, mysterious, and impulsive and they know how to get what they want. They don't change their stripes just to conform to the latest social gimmick preached in chick flicks, daytime talk shows, and slick magazines.

Sure keepers are sweet and considerate. But they also take care of business. They're willing to put their asses on the line for their woman. They understand that relationships are not about getting something. They're about giving it. That's why keeper guys are rare. How rare?

By my estimation, keepers make up about 20 percent of the available guy pool. Tops. I used to tell people during my interviews that every now and again a keeper gets released back into the pond—usually via divorce. Yet, for the most part, the pond is swimming with jerks (suckers and carp).

The uncomfortable truth is that a whole lot of women actually dig jerks. There's a sizable body of research suggesting that men with jerky personalities—narcissism, aggression, danger seeking, deviousness—score most often with women. (See "Bad Guys Really do Get the Most Girls," *New Scientist*, June 18, 2008 and *Who is James Bond?: The Dark Triad as an Agentic Social Style*, Peter K. Jonason, *New Mexico State University*.)

Researchers believe women go for jerks because a jerky attitude signals high testosterone levels. And in the dog-eat-dog environment our ancestors caroused in, abundant testosterone meant higher rates of reproductive success and family survival. That wiring thing again.

Eighty percent of available guys have some sort of personal flaw. They've been divorced twice or more. They drink too much. They can't keep a job. They talk trash in polite company. They're thoughtless and self-centered. They accumulate unmanageable debt with little to show for it. They eat dough balls. They are shaped like dough balls, etc.

How to Keep a Keeper

If a woman lands a keeper, she shows poor judgment if she releases or forces him back into the pond (though a lot of other women will be thanking her). So once she's landed one, how can she keep a keeper (assuming she really wants one)? The best guys require care and feeding. They want to be loved and admired, even on those occasions where they don't deserve it. Because most of the time your pork rind eating, sports stats-loving hunk will not be doing what (or acting like) you want.

First, a keeper doesn't want drama, not from his woman or from those close to her. Second, a keeper wants to know his woman is sincerely curious about—or at the very least respects—his passions. Third, she needs to cut him some slack every once in a while in the "feelings" department. Men are hard wired to approach things linearly. They tend to get totally absorbed in a project or task until it is completed.

Often a man is so focused on what's in front of him that he doesn't have the time or mental bandwidth for what a woman might call "polite" interactions. You know, the kind that have the "right tone." But let there be no mistake: the right men will compromise and find the time to do enough of the right stuff and say the right things to be keepers.

And finally and most importantly, most keepers likely want frequent and varied sex. Keep a keeper by giving it to him. Keepers want a woman who is sincerely willing to satisfy her man physically. Nothing replaces the feeling a man has when he is truly desired by his woman. Nothing.

So that, in short, is how you find, land and care for a keeper. Jump in. The pond water is warm. And pigs are great swimmers.

CHAPTER 7

What Can Go Wrong?

*"Eighty percent of married men cheat in
America. The rest cheat in Europe."*
— COMEDIAN JACKIE MASON

"I know nothing about sex, because I was always married."
— ACTRESS ZSA ZSA GABOR

*"A man can be short and dumpy and getting
bald, but if he has fire, women will like him."*
— MAE WEST

Relationships will not last if the basic needs of each person involved are not met. These needs might range from praise and adoration, to financial security, to a commitment, to clear communications, to a sincere interest in each other's passions. And sex.

All of those people who think sex is not important need to get over it. Now. Sex is a basic need. Among the men I interviewed who were happiest in their relationships, the most frequently cited reason for their happiness was a satisfying sex life. I did interview a few men who weren't all that interested in sex. They, of course, are a good fit for someone as well. But they don't make up a majority of men by any means.

Whatever your basic needs might be, you must tell your partner what they are in order to have any chance of having them satisfied. Expecting your partner to read your mind is a losing game played by the self-absorbed. You've got to be clear about what you need.

The reasons for breakups vary wildly. One man I interviewed revealed that, years after his divorce, his ex-wife told him that if she had it to do over again she would still be married to him. She said that in hindsight the problems that led to their breakup were not as big a deal as she thought at the time. Had he been able to get her to tell him what she needed and given him the chance to satisfy those needs, he said, they could have saved the relationship.

As we get older, we should gain the wisdom to pick our battles and to be more tolerant of each other. With any luck, we discover that many of the things that bothered us when we were younger aren't that important in the long run.

Kids go away. Our financial and career situation improves. And with these changes many other stressful factors cease to be issues. So, in theory, it should be easier for older folks to focus on each other later in life.

Unfortunately, by the time wisdom arrives, the relationship may be so badly damaged that we are not interested in making it work with the original spouse.

Sometimes it is not weariness, but the fantasy of greener grass that wrecks a long-term relationship. Guys and girls get infatuated with the idea of a new partner. So much exciting stuff goes on in a new relationship. It's so easy to get sucked in by new mysteries, new discoveries, and new sex. Working on the fundamentals of an existing relationship is hard work and might seem dull by comparison. If you are beginning to fantasize about a new partner, think a little about what might be causing those thoughts.

Stabbed by Jealousy

Jealousy is a big problem in far too many relationships. Many women (and men) are intensely jealous and possessive. Now a small amount of jealousy is flattering. But when it turns into obsession or chronic distrust, it's poison; it's a disease that's difficult to cure.

One man I interviewed told me his wife constantly combed through his computer, cell phone, and phone bill. She was on the hunt for evidence of cheating. It got so bad he was forced to close his Facebook account after his wife discovered girls he knew from high school had friended him on Facebook. She came unglued. (Although they reconnect old friends, Facebook and other social media sites can wreak havoc on relationships that involve men or women prone to jealousy.)

A Word about Facebook

 I found a number of people who experienced friction in their relationships or had gotten a divorce over issues surrounding Facebook. From stoking jealousies in a mate by reconnecting with a high school or college friend, to using relationship status (i.e., single, in a relationship, married, etc.) as a weapon by changing it immediately after a fight, Facebook is loaded with relationship landmines. I found many instances of seemingly innocent postings triggering unexpected nasty reactions. Some people use Facebook to keep an eye on each other, and not necessarily in a bad way. The best rule of thumb is to carefully consider each posting and designation. For example, a lot of people leave their relationship status blank. Yet this can create angst too, as there is often pressure to move it one way or the other (certainly those who are married should indicate that). But leaving it blank seems to generate fewer problems than changing it back and forth with each new girlfriend/boyfriend or fight.

He wasn't cheating. But she would view even a harmless friend request from an old classmate as a threat. To feel secure, she wanted to know where he was, whom he was talking to, and what he was looking at on the Internet every second of every day.

Ironically, she was the one who was cheating. Her raging jealously was just her way to defend herself against the same pain that her infidelity caused him.

In a perfect world, one where mates aren't excessively jealous, conversations with someone of the opposite sex wouldn't be a problem. But if your mate is the jealous type, you have to make a reasonable effort to accommodate these insecurities. Be on your best behavior at all times so that you avoid inciting them unnecessarily.

His or her jealousy may stem from a cheating partner in a previous relationship. Invest time and effort reassuring and building up the confidence of the person you are in a relationship with. Is it a hardship? Sure. But it's what you do if you value and respect the relationship.

For some women, the jealously is so intense they get angry if their man even looks at another woman, however innocent that glance may be. Men are hard-wired to respond to female appearances. But if your turning head agitates your partner, tone it down a little to put her at ease. It's a good idea to please your mate and generate as little negative energy as possible.

Now I'm not suggesting you should stay in a relationship that requires you to continually walk on eggshells. If you're in one of those stressful relationships that is constantly being put in peril by jealousy, it may be time to ask: Is this a good fit?

After all, there's a certain amount of risk here. Jealously can be the result of a serious personality disorder. If red flags pop up in the beginning of the relationship, it will likely only get worse. You need to get ahead of it. If you discover your special someone is overly possessive and isn't able to control these impulses, it's time to move on.

I recently met a girl who had been with the same guy for two years. She said he was always a little jealous and controlling. He made her dress conservatively. He discouraged her from hanging out with her friends without him. But it didn't really bother her—until it went to the next level.

Just after the relationship hit the two-year mark, she discovered a tracking device on her car. That's jealousy turned into creepy distrust. The guy's defense when caught? He said he had installed the device so that if she were ever in an accident, he could easily locate her. How thoughtful. He refused to apologize for invading her privacy.

Looking back, she thought it was odd that he always seemed to call or text just as she was leaving someplace or making an unplanned stop. She said she had asked him twice whether he was tracking or following her, and he had lied to her both times.

That's a personality disorder. There's no moving on to the "let's be together *forever*" phase. The sooner she cuts him loose, the sooner she can recover her sanity and confidence and find a keeper. I hope she does, without guilt. Ultimately, there is someone out there for this guy, someone who won't mind the tracking (surveillance gets some people hot) or the matronly clothes.

Question: Why do women stay with men who have severe jealousy issues? Many say it's because they are "in love." But how can staying with a controlling, jealous schlub that carps about a woman's whereabouts and dress all of the time be considered "love?"

By the way, I want to make one distinction here. Simple jealousy is one thing. It may be manageable. You can be jealous, even competitive, without going psycho. But when it becomes pathological distrust, it's a cancer. It's dangerous.

How'd I End up with 40 Miles of Rough Road?

"It seems like everybody gets fat," a man told me during one of my interview sessions. "I've got to tell you, before I went to my 40-year high school reunion; I'd never seen so many ugly people together in one place. I couldn't believe it. It made me feel so good about the way I look."

It's true. When people get comfortable in their relationships, they take them for granted. They let the part about working to please the other person go by the wayside. They get lazy and let themselves go. Or maybe they feel like once they've bagged a mate, looking good isn't necessary or worth the bother.

It sometimes seems that when women hit 40, they take out their breast implants, throw out their thongs, cut their hair, and sentence their spiky heels to the back of the closet. Then they don't understand why men don't give them the attention they once did. Newsflash: Most men are attracted to women with big breasts, sexy skirts, really tall spiky heels, thong panties (or none), and long hair. Sorry. Call me a pig. Call all of us pigs. Men love these feminine features and accessories.

Deep down women know this. That's why after they get that divorce they lose weight, start wearing heels and thong panties, and let their hair grow out, and even get implants. (When men split up, they pluck the lint from their navels, pick up their clothes, launder their socks, and wash and put away the dishes. And mind their belching.)

There are very, very few men who don't consider a woman's overall look a big deal. A man may say to a woman that physical appearance doesn't matter, but he's lying. He is afraid to tell her the truth for fear of hurting her feelings or unleashing her wrath. You pig! (You mean you don't love me anymore because I gained 40 pounds? What man wants to have that conversation?)

It's very important for a man to be with a woman he finds physically attractive. A woman who puts effort into making herself look great is essentially saying to her man: *hey, I'm really in to you.* He makes note of it, even if only subconsciously.

But uncorking this issue with most women is risky. The age of 40 is a big milestone for most women. So is 50. They often feel like they're washed up, that nobody wants them anymore. Their childbearing years are behind them. They feel fat, wrinkled, saggy and otherwise a mess.

So men must do everything they can to make their women feel better about themselves. Figure out ways to inspire her to take an interest in her looks. You could say: "Wow, you still have a great figure. I'd like to see more of it." Never miss an opportunity to praise a woman's manner of dress, her hair, and her shoes. Tell her she looks great in that pair of sweats and tank top. It's really not that hard. You might be surprised at the dividends you earn (BJTCs galore).

And men? Women are far more forgiving of a man's looks than the other way around. If a man is financially responsible and his woman loves and respects him, she'll grant him a lot of leeway in the looks department. And yes, there is a double standard here.

Still, women like men who open their door, send flowers, regularly shower, brush their teeth, and keep their fingernails clean and trimmed (for starters). (Keeping one's fingernails clean and smooth says to a woman: *Hey, I'm really in to you.*) They like a man who minds his paunch. Women also like men who are stylish. Yet very few men are. That's why women often buy men most of their clothes. Hey, why are you guys having your women buy your clothes?

Fact is, women like men who like to shop. But most men hate shopping. My advice? Get over it. Compromise. Learn to shop. A little can go a long way. If you're dating and you're interested in attracting a good woman, you need to work at being stylish. Plus, you will feel better about yourself because you know she thinks you look good. If you do, you'll set yourself far apart from the rest of the pigs who think spicy pork rinds make for great cologne.

We all will diligently work on ourselves for a new woman or a new man. The sad thing is we will do things to please them we would never do for our spouses or long-term partners. So try thinking of your significant other as a new dating prospect. Understand that in long-term relationships, we need to recharge each other's batteries by regularly sexing up our habits and appearance. And you can't recharge the batteries by sitting on the couch, loading up on carbs, and watching *Swamp People.*

Insults: Poisoning the Well

Another symptom of relationships stuck in the taken-for-granted pit is we grow comfortable making offhanded or snide remarks about—or to—our partners. The sad truth is that we sometimes direct remarks toward our spouses or partners that we would never dream of directing toward others. Yet we do it. And it's so wrong. It's very hard to repair a relationships wounded by name-calling and verbal abuse.

Booze often plays a role in this. As relationships wear on, some of us become drinkers to relieve the monotony. And when people drink they sometimes become verbally abusive among other things. Booze-induced hostility is a major cause of breakups, especially among younger people who haven't gotten all of the partying out of their systems. I would say that 50 percent of relationship splits among my interviewees were caused or hastened by too much alcohol.

Couples also need to be cognizant of a woman's monthly cycles, especially if she has behavior issues associated with hormones. Women should discuss this with their partners and keep them informed. You can both mark the dates on your calendars so you don't overact to situations—or over-act to overreactions—and say something you will regret.

A good rule of thumb: Always strive to make each other look good whenever and wherever possible. Even

You look good. I look good. We all look good.

I learned an important lesson in business from a consultant who trained my staff in successful interpersonal relations in the workplace. "Always make me look good, and I will always make you look good. In the end, we will both look good." Too often, especially early in a relationship, we may say negative things about our partner to those closest to us to let off steam. Oftentimes, these comments aren't totally justified, or are just plain wrong. At a minimum our one-sided perspective colors them. In these situations, those closest to us will seldom hear all the good things about our partner, only the bad things. So they swiftly form a negative opinion of our partner.

Is it any wonder then that our closest confidants don't seem to like our partner? In worst-case scenarios, these perceptions never turn around. Have you ever had someone say something snide about your mate? Did you let it go? Or did you correct them on the spot? You will find that if you immediately defend your mate and take the opportunity to make them look good by pointing out why you appreciate them, those nasty comments will stop. Not only that, but by vocalizing your appreciation your own perceptions will change, for the better. You'll discover that this positive energy is *very* contagious. Everyone looks good!

when a relationship is on the skids, make the effort to cast each other in a positive light. Never—ever—intentionally embarrass your spouse or partner in public. Humiliating your partner in front of others cuts to the bone. It's almost worse than cheating.

I learned this in business. (Remember, I said my business lessons were applied in many ways to this book, however unromantic that is.) If I make you look good, and you make me look good, we will always look good to others. From a purely selfish standpoint, making someone else look bad in public makes *you* look like an ass. Handle the dirty laundry when you get home. Keep it civil and just between the two of you.

The Difficult Years

It's a wonder any of us stay together for more than a few years when you really think about it. After we get married, we invest so much time and energy in our kids and our careers. We get hit with financial turmoil. We may experience a few layoffs. There are issues with in-laws, neighbors, and the kids as they morph into aliens, otherwise known as teenagers. How could we possibly devote time to each other? How could we ever have time for sex?

It's no surprise that after 10 or 15 years we end up taking each other for granted. We convince ourselves we were there for the kids. But what happens when the kids leave? Suddenly, we're face to face with a person we've neglected for decades. Oops.

What Can Go Wrong?

I was listening to a radio show recently and one of the guests said that if we somehow just made all of the women younger, thinner, and with bigger boobs, we wouldn't need Viagra. Men who had been married for years would be in love again. While this may have some merit, in reality men just want to be chased—and surprised. At least according to the men I interviewed.

In the long run, women and men both take each other for granted. We stop making compromises. We don't kiss anymore. We lose our enthusiasm for sex. When the relationship was new, and he wanted to have sex in a public restroom (isn't that why they created "family" restrooms?), she eagerly agreed. She may have even suggested it!

She would have sex in the morning—*anytime* in the morning. But as the years wore on, she stopped chasing him and wouldn't even consider a quickie after her morning shower. "I don't want to smell like sex all day," she would say. Not so when the relationship was new. Then she was eager for such trysts, and would just hop back into the shower and use the handheld showerhead for a quickie freshener (and maybe a little excitement).

Early on, all couples swear they will never fall into the trap of taking each other for granted. Yet it invariably creeps up on them over time. Few of those couples in relationships for more than 5 years continue having spontaneous sex in public places or lunchtime trysts in the car. And what ever happened to those impromptu blowjobs given while you're making your way through traffic? It's safer than texting. I mean texting forces you to take your eyes off the road.

Yet what happens after the breakup? Both parties start doing all of that crazy stuff with their new partner. This is one of the reasons why pigs cheat. They yearn for a taste of that old excitement (not that this justifies cheating). They decide what they really need is a wild woman for crazy sex: a ménage à trois, sex in public, strap-ons and strap-tos, leaving the lights on, and everything in between. He thinks he can't have these things with his current partner. Sometimes that's true. But he should make the effort to give it a whirl with her.

Women want that excitement too. They want passionate kissing. Don't kid yourself. It's the rare couple indeed that maneuvers around the rut of taking each other for granted.

Is Long-Term Romance Even Possible?

According to a recent study of 2,000 couples by the hotel chain Travelodge, 90 percent of couples don't say "I love you" before turning out the lights at night. Some 80 percent don't kiss each other goodnight and 54 percent sleep with their backs toward each other. A quarter of the couples in the study say they don't like their partner touching them while they're asleep. Talk about taking each other for granted.

Staying engaged sexually takes lots of imagination and energy. And work.

Ideally, in relationships, we balance the negative and positive energies flowing through them. But the difficult years often have lots of negative energy and nothing to offset it. What to do?

Talk to each other for starters. Learn how to get reacquainted. Be mindful of the changes that will creep up due to the aging process. Be aware that hysterectomies, antidepressants, and other medications can diminish sex drive (see Chapter 8). Never underestimate the value of a change of scenery, of getting away, even over short distances for brief periods. We've got to force ourselves to have sex during these difficult years.

Sex brings closeness. It reenergizes us and revitalizes our relationships during the difficult years. Sex does for relationships what bacon does for appetites. Oink oink.

Strategic Breakups

 One of the men I interviewed recalled the moment he realized his life had changed. He was sitting on a porch in Pebble Beach. He was about to turn 50. He was suddenly aware of life's goal post. "I don't want to spend the rest of my life doing what I'm doing," he remembered saying. "Yet I was violently opposed to divorce. But once you've decided that the person you are with is not the person you want to spend the rest of your life with,

every hour—every moment—together is a waste of time."
His life was two-thirds over and he realized it.

In situations like this, you feel like you've got to get out
as soon as you can. You don't care anymore. You no longer
have the energy to fight the battles. Still, once faced with
this realization, many of us wait too long to leave. Only
when the pain of staying exceeds the pain of leaving do
we break away. The fear of the unknown strikes again.

No matter when you decide to leave, do it only after
you've exhausted all of your options. Don't be reckless about
it. Break up strategically. By giving thought to your split,
you will likely avoid a whole lot of nastiness and costly
emotional and financial chaos.

What do I mean by breaking up strategically? Once
many of the men I interviewed decided they wanted a
divorce, they just marched home and barked out of the
blue: "I want a divorce." The woman was shocked. It was
like a slap in the face. There was no warning. And these
men were flabbergasted when the split went poorly. (Note:
According to a 2004 national survey by AARP, women
initiate most of the breakups in the golden years. Among
those between the ages 40-69, women reported seeking
divorce 66 percent of the time.)

In most instances when relationships turn sour, no
one wants to step up to hold out the olive branch. No one
is willing to declare a truce. They get hung up on who's at
fault. But you need to seek peace, no matter who is at fault.

My advice: Lose the disagreeable attitude. Scorching each other's earth only affects everyone negatively—including the kids—and adversely affects one's ex's ability to honor financial obligations in the future.

During my interviews, I suggested to one woman who was having marital problems that she go home and give her husband a BJTC. She did. He was shocked. On day two, I suggested she march home and give him another BJTC. By now, he was suspicious. On day three . . . well, you know the rest.

She softened him up. Now he would be ready to hear her talk about how she wanted to please him, how she wanted to make sure they were together forever. If after all of that effort he didn't eventually respond favorably, he was no longer a keeper. She could feel free to move on. And the best part? She could leave the relationship with no regrets. Not to mention that she is experienced and knowledgeable on how to please that new guy. He'll bury her in flowers.

It's also a good idea to seek counseling. Now many men refuse to go through counseling. They think it's a waste of time. But this attitude is shortsighted because these men might actually get something out of it. If you get nothing else from counseling, you might at least end up having a friendlier divorce. And don't be afraid to go by yourself if necessary so you can have a "no regrets" outcome.

Example: One of the men I interviewed agreed to counseling with his wife and they stuck with it for two years. At the two-year mark the counselor suddenly announced:

"You know what? We've been meeting for two years, and we don't seem to be making a lot of progress. We don't seem to be able to compromise on the core issues. I think we should start talking about collaborative divorce." The counselor said the "D" word first, not the spouses. After a few sessions with some crying, things progressed to a friendly split. He and his ex-wife are good friends to this day.

The lesson: If you absolutely must get a divorce, be patient, go through counseling, and be thoughtful and fair throughout the process. You will avoid a lot of unnecessary spite and have a much better outcome.

Now if you get caught cheating, all bets are off.

CHAPTER 8

Navigating the
Menopause Minefield

*"An archaeologist is the best husband a woman can have;
the older she gets the more interested he is in her."*

— BRITISH CRIME WRITER AGATHA CHRISTIE

If your wife or girlfriend is 40 or older, or has
had a partial or full hysterectomy, you had
better get ready to grab yourself by the ass. Because you
may be in for the ride of your life, if all of my interviews
are accurate.

Nearly 80 percent of the people I interviewed over the
age of 40 were divorced. (Since 1990, the divorce rate has
doubled among people ages 50 and older according to *The
Gray Divorce Revolution* by Susan Brown and I-Fen Lin of
Bowling Green State University.) Some had remarried. Half
of the men I spoke with told me that failure to deal with
menopause was the big reason for their divorces.

Menopause is that time in a woman's life when her ovaries gradually shut down. Think of it as the beginning of the end of the childbearing chapter. It's the time in her life when a woman must say goodbye to the young, fertile woman she once was. Kids leaving home to go to college or make a way for themselves makes this whole chapter even more difficult. It makes a woman feel as through time really *is* catching up to her.

Many women are highly sensitive about their age. As they pass 40, then 50 they think they aren't desirable anymore. This dovetails with and aggravates menopause.

But this isn't the whole story. What triggers this process is the gradual halting of the release of the hormones that regulate fertility cycles. The loss of these hormones not only brings on physical symptoms like hot flashes, night sweats, insomnia, occasional bouts of rapid heart rate, and itching, but also can touch off huge swings in personality and behavior. (Research shows that women who exercise, are not overweight, and are generally in good health are better equipped to handle menopause.)

The dramatic shifts in behavior happen because the hormones that regulate the physical parts of the fertility cycle affect moods too. These hormones also drive a woman's urge to nurture and help her tune into the feelings of others. When these hormones are cut off, all hell breaks loose. She can cry for no reason. She can go from sweet and serene to crazed monster at the flip of a switch.

These swings can scare the living crap out of a man because he never knows who he will be dealing with from moment to moment. (Some women have little or no adverse effects from menopause, but I didn't find many.)

Women who undergo hysterectomies also show these hair-raising swings. But the shift can be more dramatic because the hormones get cut off instantly—with the flick of a scalpel. One of the men I interviewed had been married for many years and he and his wife had always enjoyed a fantastic relationship.

Then she had a hysterectomy. It changed her from her teeth to her toenails. She could go from pleasant to violent in an instant. She would break into crying fits for no reason. But here's what was odd about this: She had no idea she was behaving this way. She was completely unaware that she had changed.

Another man I interviewed decided to leave his girlfriend of ten years because her personality changed so dramatically—from sweet and even to erratic and nasty. She was as mean as a bulldog. They discovered her changes in behavior were because of menopause, a realization that came too late to prevent the break up.

Too Many Heads in the Sand

Based on my interviews, I've concluded that roughly 50 percent of women are in denial about the consequences of menopause. They don't think it's a problem. Either they don't realize it's happening, or they simply don't want to face it. It's a blow to the female ego. So they often refuse to talk to a doctor or get tested to determine hormone levels and treatment options.

Of the fifty percent who are not in denial, half are unwilling to consider hormone replacement therapy because of the risks (heart disease, breast cancer, and stroke according to the National Cancer Institute). That means just 25 percent of women who are facing the issue are doing something about it. Seventy-five percent are not. And most of the women in this group don't want to talk about it. And God help the man who brings it up.

 I'm convinced that a big part of dealing with menopause is just simple awareness—on the part of both partners. It's knowing that menopause is likely to bring on at least some changes in personality and mood and being ready for them. It's knowing that a woman may feel angrier or more emotional and being aware that it's possible to keep these feelings in check. A man who loves her can help her by understanding the changes that are happening to her, offering support, and treading lightly.

Here are my suggestions for easing the strain of the explosive menopause minefield:

- **Validate.** The symptoms are real. Denial is deadly. There are many tests and remedies available—there are even home use menopause test kits—so there is no reason to ignore it.
- **Be Aware.** The both of you must make every effort to think before you act and speak during this hair-trigger phase.

- **Stay Connected.** Face this change together. Be vigilant against the tendency to grow distant.
- **Humor.** Keep your sense of humor, but never, ever belittle a menopausal woman, particularly when there are sharp objects within easy reach.
- **Communicate.** Make sure you check in with each other regularly. But never ask how your mate is doing just to check the box. Ask. *Listen.* Respond with sincerity.
- **Learn.** Pursue counseling and explore books on natural or alternative remedies. Get tested.
- **Start early.** The time to discuss menopause is before she has entered this phase—age 40 or shortly there-after. Then the talks can be productive and pragmatic. If you wait until she's in full-blown menopause, you likely will be dead soon. Or wish you were.
- **Pledge.** Commit to solutions, including more sex.

This last suggestion can be a real challenge. One of the symptoms of menopause in many women is a decline in the libido. But waning interest in sex is one of the things you have to make every effort to overcome. Many of the medications prescribed for menopause are anti-depressants with known side effects, including a reduction in sexual desire.

If a woman is going to be a hellcat due to menopausal mood swings, having more sex is going to help offset that. As a man, if I can get off more, I can better tolerate my she-devil on jet fuel. If she can get off more, she will feel better about our relationship. Everything we can do to gain momentum for positive energy is going to help us successfully pass through the menopause minefield.

Macho Menopause: Low T

But it isn't just women who get stuck with the menopause curse. Men experience big age-related shifts too. As men get older, their testosterone levels decline.

Testosterone is the hormone that makes men, men. It builds muscle, bone and gives you drive. Remember when you were 15 and you were so wound up you felt like you could easily screw a shapely tree and get off? That was testosterone.

Virtually all men by middle age experience some decline in testosterone levels. Defined by experts as less than 300 nanograms per deciliter of blood, Low T can kick the pig right out of you. It can slap you with low energy, sleep disturbances, erectile dysfunction, and a slackening sex drive. Ever feel like falling asleep in the car on the way to work in the morning? Sounds like Low T.

One of the men I interviewed did everything to revive his T. He ate right, worked out, and shed his very small spare tire. Nothing worked until he tried testosterone therapy.

Many men who experience Low T have symptoms without realizing it. Fortunately, you can fix low T with testing and testosterone replacement treatments: skin gels, skin patches, tablets, or injections.

But testosterone replacement therapy won't restore the vigor you had as a randy 20-year-old if you have normal levels for your age. However, if your levels are below normal, it can work wonders.

Anything that can give you more energy is a good thing. If your testosterone levels slip below 300, you're definitely not loving life or loving much of anything else. Testosterone treatments may be the best-kept secret in town. Plus, most health insurance plans will cover testosterone treatment therapy. So read up, fuel up, and reacquaint yourself with the pig you always were.

CHAPTER 9

Tips to Make it Better
(Off to Charm School)

"Any man who can drive safely while kissing a pretty girl
is simply not giving the kiss the attention it deserves."
— ALBERT EINSTEIN

In *The Monogamy Gap: Men, Love and the Reality of Cheating,* sociologist Eric Anderson discusses the rush of oxytocin we get early on in a relationship just from cuddling with our partner on the couch, or taking a walk. We don't get this same rush from actual sex.

As the relationship goes on, Anderson explains, the excitement and passion pales in comparison to what was felt when a couple was first getting acquainted. In fact, the excitement in most relationships tapers off after just 6 months.

Everyone insists at the beginning they won't be one those statistics. But it's a tough road. Only those couples willing to discuss and deal with their needs and desires can beat the odds and keep the torch alive, albeit with a smaller flame.

 There are many available strategies—or big picture plans—for reaching your relationship goals and keeping that torch ablaze. It's probably best for the two of you to collaborate and devise your own strategies based on personal preferences and personality types. Below, I've supplied a few tactics—or short-term actions—to help drive your strategy to reach your goals.

- Be aware of the optics of presentation. Frame criticisms and suggestions in ways that make the other person feel better. For example, instead of blurting out that your mate is overweight, tell him or her you would love to see their great physique or figure again. Or tell them you are going on a diet to look your best.
- Give up your right to be offended. Sure, the occasional tone of your partner's voice or roll of the eyes might annoy you. My advice: if these aren't chronic occurrences, give it up already. Being offended is more often than not a selfish act borne of self-righteousness. We get miffed because someone said or did something without taking our feelings into consideration. We need to get over ourselves.
- Kill them with kindness for 30 days. Keep a leash on your irritation. The very first time you get angry at your partner, the 30-day count starts over. The very first time you catch yourself making a snide remark, the

count starts over. Do everything your partner wants. Don't ask for anything. Then watch the magic happen.

- Focus on romance. Women don't separate sex from romance. Men do (that wiring thing again). But for a woman if there is no romance, sex just becomes routine—and desire gradually fades away. And romance isn't just buying stuff. It's non-sexual affection: an unexpected kiss or hug or a pinch or an arm on the small of her back. The more attention and caring you show a woman, the more you will get laid. There is no substitute for flowers, cards, candy and an occasional teddy bear. If you are not sending flowers every 8 weeks, with cards more regularly, you have totally blown it.

- Be willing to compromise. But a key to successful compromising is having a firm grasp of your core values and issues. Compromising on things that are important to you leads to resentment. Be firm, but be realistic in your expectations.

- Force yourself to have more sex. I am convinced that men have to have it in most cases. Women get benefits as well. It's much cheaper than lawyers.

- Laugh. Find each other's funny bones and exploit them shamelessly.

- Be curious about your partner. Ask: What makes you feel good? What makes you feel comfortable? What energizes you? What is the most significant thing I don't understand about your sexuality?

- Be willing to extend the olive branch, even when you're sure you're right. Isn't taking the hit now and then worth the extra nooky? So many folks I interviewed have said that, in hindsight, they could have resolved their issues had they worried less about who was at fault.

- Give Pedestal Treatment a chance(see Chapter 10)
- Plan for sex. Put it on your calendar. Prepare for it like you would a special occasion. Make it an adventure. Share fantasies.
- Practice Tolerance. Couples must tolerate the quirks and failings of each other if they hope to stay together. Some things may not be as easy to overlook or to tolerate as others. But it's vital to learn to deal with petty annoyances so that you can focus on what's important. Again, know your core values so you don't confuse what matters with what doesn't.
- Embrace a "no regrets" strategy. Never look back and say, "damn, if only I hadn't said/done that." Accept it and move on. Then plan things so you never have a sense of regret.
- Be chivalrous. Hold open doors, walk on the outside of the sidewalk, rise when a woman enters or exits a room, etc. It's the best-kept scoring secret—it's a competitive edge that wins every time.
- Chase your man. Men like that. (We know women like it.) If you don't think other single women will flirt with or chase the guy you've got your eye on, you are delusional.
- Stoke Desire. If either of you notice a waning or lack of sexual desire, explore the reasons and take action immediately. Lack of desire destroys relationships.

To the more highly sexed spouse, sex is about feeling wanted and loved and emotionally connected. Cut that off and the relationship will slowly wither. Low testosterone levels, menopause, and medications such as antidepressants and treatments for cardiovascular conditions can dampen desire. So does neglecting your physical appearance. Talk about it. Consult a doctor or therapist. Join a gym and buy some sexy shoes and short skirts. Get on it and get it on!

- Give her a bath.
- Blindfold and kidnap her for a surprise night in a hotel.
- Consider a PMS calendar (you may want to keep one without discussing it. If you discuss it she may help you pinpoint the dates).
- Don't blame every one of her outbursts on PMS.
- Give each other enough space to pursue separate activities, interests and relationships.
- Exercise. It increases sex drive.
- Run your fingers through her hair.
- Listen. Make eye contact. Nod your head. Clarify key points by repeating them back and confirming your understanding. Hear each other out. Listening says, "I love you."
- Men: wear a well-tailored suit (don't have one? Get one) every once in a while. It drives them wild.
- Commit to making each other the center of attention for a day, a week, a month—until it sticks.
- Guy's night out. Many girls often have girl's nights. Guys need them too. We all need room to unleash our

gender wiring in a safe, friendly zone. One guy told me he gets great sex the night before his guy's night out so that his girl is sure that he doesn't forget what he has. A little bit of absence makes the heart grow fonder. Other things too.

• Upgrade. Expand your horizons. Go to museums, plays, concerts, parks and libraries. Go on hikes. Ride your bikes. Rollerblade. Bird watch. Go camping. Hump in a tent.

No matter what tactics you use, the key to long-term success is persistence. Experiment with these tips and develop new ones as new challenges enter your relationship. You might want to keep a running list.

The important thing is to keep the positive energy flowing. And the best way to keep the energy and juices flowing is make sex the foundation of your tip sheet. You'll be happier than a pig in sh . . . , er sheets. And that ain't no hogwash.

CHAPTER 10

How to Keep Them—Forever

*"A successful man is one who makes more
money than his wife can spend. A successful
woman is one who can find such a man."*

— Actress Lana Turner

Woman and men want relationships for different reasons. Women want security—and not necessarily financial security, especially these days. More often, they want emotional security. A woman needs to know her man is thinking of her, that he remembers the little things she likes and dislikes. And acts on them. Above all, she wants her man to show he is paying attention to her and her alone, not just paying. A woman hates to compete for her man's attention with a television, a cell phone, or an iPad. Turn those off and turn her on.

But keep in mind: Women are constantly rating you. Past deeds don't count. It's what you've done for her lately that counts.

Men want to feel admired. They want their passions, talents and knowledge to be appreciated by their women. They like it when a woman asks them for advice. And men want their physical needs tended to. They want plenty of sex. And just like women, men like to be chased.

As I have said, men and women are wired differently. For one thing, with women sex starts at the brain and works its way down—slowly. For men, sex starts at the penis (often triggered by visual stimuli) and makes its way up to the brain—rapidly, although sometimes it gets stuck en route. And unlike women, men generally don't like to spend a lot of time talking about relationships.

Also, until recently at least, girls were conditioned from an early age to be attentive and accommodating (this could be as much nature as nurture). That's why women seem attuned to the needs of others, as if by instinct.

Not so with men. Men generally don't knock their heads against their beer cans trying to figure out what other people want or need. And they hate the guessing games and demands that they be mind readers. They need to be told. Specifically. And it's not because men are selfish or dim-witted. It's because they're wired to respond to what's literal and direct. Once women accept that men are wired differently and stop trying to change their men into women with facial stubble, they can make progress.

Still, with these hard-wired differences in mind, if men want better relationships with women, they have to think more strategically about what they say and do. Men often get into trouble because they misread the signals that women send after certain fights, the serious kind that send her to the corner of the room in tears. After a long talk and perhaps some make-up sex, a man thinks everything is fine. He thinks the issue is resolved. She knows it's not.

After those fights that reduce a woman to tears, she is the one who decides when everything is all right again. Until she says it's fixed, it's not fixed. And remember she may not literally say it's fixed. Listen carefully to what she says and how she says it. Tune into her non-verbal cues. Any argument a man thinks is over is likely not over.

Of course, if she says it's fixed when it's really not, she's messing with your wiring. Call her out on it. Explain what "fixed" means to the male brain. Don't be snide, but share with her how your male wiring means you look at things in a completely different way.

These differences between the sexes are not right or wrong. They're just what *is*. Learn to deal with them. Once you understand the basic differences in male-female wiring and tend to them, great things begin to happen.

Working the Wiring

I interviewed an older guy whom I'd bet most who met him would figure he'd be dead last on the list of those "most likely to be a chick magnet." He's not rich. He drives a hauler for a living. He's not particularly handsome either. Far from it. In fact, you could go so far as to say he's uglier than a bucket full of armpits.

But: he has an intuitive sense of female wiring. And the women flock to him.

"You would not believe how many attractive women in their late 40's and 50's there are out there," he told me. "They're all divorced. Kids are grown and gone. They don't have anyone; they don't have a companion. And they don't have any security."

 So he sets about putting them at ease. He buys them dinner. He's attentive and assuring. He keeps in touch. He takes care of business. This is working the wiring at the fundamental level. It doesn't take much. And he isn't taking advantage of these women. He's sincerely satisfying some of their most basic needs. He reports that he gets laid regularly.

From here you can layer on the particulars. Despite what the "grrrl power" movement wants you to think, women love old-fashioned chivalry. They get irritated if you don't open the door for them. They appreciate it when you get up from your seat as they leave the table to freshen up in the ladies' room. They melt when you put your hand in the small of their back to guide them across the street or through the door. They love holding hands on the couch.

How to Keep Them—Forever

One girl I interviewed "fired" her man after the first date because he didn't buy her a flower from a street vendor they'd bumped into. Maybe that's overkill. But what's the downside to these little gestures? Her belief was that it would only go downhill from that first date. And if he can't do it on the first date, well . . .

Women adore little spontaneous touches. Like messages in cards. A bouquet of flowers clipped from the yard or picked up at the grocery store to go with that bottle of wine. Backrubs and/or foot rubs too. Even a hard-charging, successful type A female executive still needs nurturing. Lots of it.

For example, women like a man who knows how to maneuver through an airport, how to move through security quickly and get the best seats for the flight. Nothing impresses a woman more than a man who is willing to tip (or bribe) the doorman at a hot nightclub to get to the front of the line. Or slip the hostess or concierge a generous gratuity to secure seats in a fully booked restaurant, avoiding the one-hour wait. It radiates a level of confidence that is highly attractive.

Most women are used to standing in line with their man to get into that hot spot. Or waiting for Tuesday night to roll around to dine at that new "it" restaurant. It blows a woman away when a man has the balls to wave a couple of twenties in front of the right people to make her feel special. Women are impressed with a man who isn't afraid to work the system for her benefit.

Women are Irresistibly
Attracted to a Man
Who Radiates Acres of
Confidence.

Women also like men who are confident in bed. Most women haven't had the pleasure of being with a man loaded with sexual swagger, one who gives instructions and is willing to try new things. Like sex in different rooms, different cars, different yards, and on different beaches, in different positions, using different furniture.

Still, the main reason most men don't get enough good sex is they don't provide "Pedestal Treatment."

Pedestal Treatment

One piece of tender loving care women (and men) may not even know they're missing is the experience of being put up on a pedestal (as I said in the introduction, this is where this book had its roots.) In the old fairy tales, chivalry meant putting well-bred women on pedestals as a way of idolizing them. Today some men claim to honor women by putting them on pedestals and calling them "princess," kind of a throwback to those tales.

Now I'm not talking about taking those fairy tales literally. Worshiping a woman as if she's infallible is stupid. If you never disagree with her, voice your desires, make suggestions that clash with hers, never say no, or continually apologize, she'll think you're a creepy beta weenie. She will treat you with contempt.

Pedestal treatment is none of that. It's an awareness that you're fortunate. It's continually wooing long after the infatuation has worn off. Love is more *doing* than it is *feeling* when you get right down to it. It's taking care of your own wiring by tending to your partner's wiring. Pedestal Treatment is how you keep things alive and kicking. And the earth moving.

Put simply, Pedestal Treatment is getting out of bed each morning with the intention of earning your lover's loyalty for one more day. Talking about it is important. Tell your partner what you are doing, and ask them what it will take for you to merit their continued devotion. Simply ask, "What can I do to keep you one more day?"

The Pedestal Treatment discussion shows you are committed to working every day to keep things hopping. It's also a good way to determine compatibility. If your lover is turned off by it, or thinks you're manipulating them, maybe the relationship doesn't have a future.

You might say, "You know what honey? I love you more than anybody else in the whole wide world. I want to be with you forever. We've been together for a long time and I know our relationship has frayed somewhat. So I want to know how I can be a better lover and companion. How can I earn your love for one more day? What can I do to make the day special for you? What can I do tomorrow? And the next day?"

Do it unconditionally. Don't expect a *quid pro quo*. Do it for 30 days and see if your situation doesn't magically shift. In all likelihood, your lover will start asking you the same questions.

If your mate doesn't respond, maybe it really is too late. But let's hope not. The beauty of Pedestal Treatment is you will almost never have to ask for what you want or need. It will just materialize. Think of it as a double shot of oink oink.

CHAPTER **11**

Pedestal Tokens:
Women and Pigs in Rehab

"I think men who have a pierced ear are better prepared for marriage. They've experienced pain and bought jewelry."

— ACTRESS AND COMEDIENNE RITA RUDNER

The *Pigs* token system is modeled on the medallion reminder systems used in many successful treatment and self-help regimens. It's designed to help you develop habits to improve your relationships and put some jet fuel in your sex life.

Pledging to do something for 30 days—without fail—is a powerful growth tool. It works because you're not getting psyched-out by the thought of making a change and having to stick with it for the rest of your life. You're testing a new habit for just a short time. If you don't like the habit after 30 days, drop it.

Yet aside from one or two items, the Pedestal Treatment system isn't designed to saddle you with a whole new set of habits anyway. What fun is that? The goal is to give you a new outlook on sex and relationships. You'll notice big changes after faithfully working with just two or three tokens. You'll do a double take on that new hot, loving partner (either existing and remade or really new) that has suddenly come into your life to mess up the sheets.

These tokens really weren't that hard to create or conceive. They just required a little thought. As mammals with above average intelligence, pigs are good at that.

Girls, you know that guy you are with? The one you think is a jerk? A pig? A perv? Just imagine—hypothetically—what that new guy you might meet at the bar or on Match.com is going to want. Your guy isn't any different from that guy in all likelihood.

Guys, do you really think all that stuff she wants is unreasonable? Imagine what that new GF is going to want. Now it's possible you may not patch things up with this system, but you're going to have fun trying. At a minimum—and this is key—you won't have any regrets. You gave it your best shot. And the best part may be that you are now trained to know what that new BF or GF is going to want.

But beware of the risks of seeking greener grass. In business, it costs 10 times as much to find a new customer as it does to keep an existing one. This same holds true in relationships. It's much less expensive in terms of time, resources and emotional outlays to make your current partner happy than to find a new one.

Punch out the token of your choice and keep it with you for the assigned period as a reminder of the change you wish to make. Then move on to the next token. Think of it as the "tokens-to-pig-heaven" get-rich-quick scheme. There is a set of tokens for women, and another for men. You may find it easier to start with the tokens that require fewer days to complete.

WHAT MOST MEN WANT

We're Looking For a few Thin, Young, PReTTY, but exTRemeLy LaRGe-bReasTed women wiTh GOOd sOCiaL skiLLs whO Know how TO COOK & CLEAN, FOR a NiCe shaLLOw ReLaTiONshiP.

Men's Tokens

Pedestal Treatment (7 days)
Every morning ask your partner "What can I do for you to earn you for one more day?"

Domestic Duties (30 days)
You know what she wants. Do it. Take out the trash. Put fresh flowers in the vases. Pick up your socks. Pick out your own clothes when dressing or shopping. Feed the dogs. Exceed her expectations.

Message Therapy (30 days)
Pepper her with surprise texts, emails, IM's, hidden notes (in her daily planner or underwear drawer if she wears any), snail mail cards and letters, racy pix, and phone calls. Message her somehow at least once per day.

Dates to Unexpected Places. (30 days, at least once weekly)
If you're in a date rut limited to restaurants, bars and movie theaters, devote the next 30 days to digging out. Try visiting a museum, an amusement park, botanical gardens, or an art gallery. Try the bathtub, a walking tour, a play, a park or a country field for stargazing. Hike a nature trail. Visit a jazz club, a zoo, a farmers' market, or the mall for some shopping and people ogling. Better yet, make it a trip. I planned a trip once for my GF, and told her to pack a coat and swimsuit. She didn't know where we were going until we got to the airport. Scottsdale. Massages. Horseback

riding. Hot air balloon rides. Paid off in spades for me in the bedroom. Both on the trip and when we got home.

Venting. Stop whining and complaining. (30 days)
No negative energy. None. Nada. Cap it. Put a sock in your pie hole. Make it all positive energy.

Unexpected Romance (4 weeks, at least once weekly)
Give her unexpected flowers (even a single stem clipped from the yard on your way in the door), a CD of her favorite recording artist, or greeting at the door with a glass of Champagne and rose-petal confetti. Get tickets. Put a rose in your teeth. Put new earrings on her while she's asleep. Kidnap her for a quick detour to a hotel, picnic, ice cream parlor, sunset in the park, or a motel with those vibrating beds. By the way, in my interviews I found lots of girls who weren't getting. . . . well, their, er . . . twat licked enough. There I said it. If she likes it—and most do—DO IT. If you don't like it, focus on pleasing her, not on the act.

Listen. (10 days)
Take time to listen. Don't turn on the TV. Or if you must, tune it to her favorite shows. Show her you can be attentive.

WHAT MOST WOMEN WANT

WE'RE LOOKING FOR A FEW RICH, TALL, DARK & HANDSOME & VERY STRONG, BUT REAL SENSITIVE MEN WHO AREN'T AFRAID OF INTIMACY, & CAN GUESS WHAT WE WANT WITHOUT HAVING TO BE TOLD WHAT IT IS.

Women's Tokens

Cook his favorite meal (7 days)
Or pick it up. He may not think much of it the first night. But on the second night, he will know something is up.

Start Sex (7 days)
Shock him. Slide over beside him on the couch. (You know, like you would do if you divorced your current man and got a new BF). Now slide your hand over onto his crotch. Tell him how much you want to restore that old spark. I'm sure you can figure out what to do next.

Relentless Sex (30 days)
Pledge to yourself to have sex at least once a day, every day, for the next 30 days. Without fail. Squeeze it in on busy days with nooners, closet rendezvous, car nooky, office trysts, early morning wake up rumbles (set the alarm 30 minutes early), lawn screws, and shower shags. Have sex in any and every location except the bedroom. And girls, you know those things you used to do? The ones a new BF would require? He gets those to. You know what he wants. Shock him. Exceed his expectations. Blow his mind (pun intended).

Fantasies (10 days)
Make it part of the relentless sex if you want. When was the last time you met him at the door with just an overcoat

on? Or cooked him dinner in the buff? Or dished-up naked breakfast?

Venting (30 days)
No whining and complaining. No negative energy. None. Not allowed. Make it all sweetness and light. No matter what.

Lose the PGS (30 days)
Go read Chapter 5. Stop doing all of that crap.

Dates to Unexpected Places (30 days, at least once weekly)
If you're in a date rut limited to restaurants, bars and movie theaters, devote the next 30 days to digging out. Try visiting a shooting range, a paintball park, a car show, a go-kart track, a fishing tournament or gun show, or the local horseracing track. Rent an exotic car. (You know what he wants while you're riding in the car don't you?)

CHAPTER 12

One Final Oink

He used to be very kind, in his own crude way
He wasn't always like I wanted him to be
He wasn't smart. He wasn't handsome either
But he thrilled me when he drilled me
and I never loved a monster quite like he . . .

— VOCALIST THANA HARRIS PERFORMING
FRANK ZAPPA'S FLAMBAY

So, there you have it, the *Men are Pigs* mani-
festo. For the men reading this book, my
hope is to give you a better understanding and appreciation
of your nature. Be proud to be a pig. As men, we shouldn't
feel the need to apologize for who we are.

Now that doesn't mean we should indulge our natures
and let them run wild. But we shouldn't suppress them
either. After all, those are the traits that women—deep
down—love most about us. Now go have some fun. Use

some of the lists and tools as a practical system to deepen your current relationships, form new, more fulfilling ones, or just get your rocks off.

If you're a woman and you've read this book all the way to this point, you're to be commended. You're open-minded and interested in pleasing your man. You've probably read some stuff here that pissed you off, yet you continued to read.

Perhaps you will approach and think about your guy differently. I hope that you will be rewarded and enjoy far more satisfying relationships because you understand men, how they think, and how to ask for what you want in ways that even a pig can understand.

I said at the start this book is from a man's perspective. I know some of the women who have made it to this point are probably gritting their teeth. Still, my hope is that you learned something you can apply to your relationships.

If not, consider a book written from a woman's perspective. With luck and research, you'll find one with thoughtful ways both men and women can relate to each other in more positive ways.

It's impossible to deny the sexes are each hard-wired differently (say it again, porker). This is a good thing. The wiring is complementary. It's how we survived all of these tens of thousands of years hunting, gathering and building. All it will take is a modest breakdown in society (a very real possibility) to bring the necessity of these differences into plain view. Should we suffer a future long-term blackout in winter, we all will appreciate how good men are at splitting logs, digging latrines, and protecting the homestead from violent invaders.

Chalking up these differences to simple knuckle-dragging selfishness doesn't make them go away. Denial of them only widens the distance between us and makes it harder for us to love and care for each other.

Of course there will be lots of women who will squeal like stuck pigs at the suggestions presented here. That's okay. We like pigs, even squealing ones.

You can even call us pigs if you wish. We don't mind. Pigs are smart. Pigs are resourceful. Pigs are very popular. The movie *Babe* (story about a piglet that aspires to be a sheepdog) earned more than $250 million at the box office and was nominated for seven Academy Awards. That's some serous ham and bacon.

And who doesn't love bacon? Not that we will let you turn us into bacon. Well, maybe we will. For a BJTC. Oink oink.

About the Author

Ron Sturgeon is a classic American entre-preneur. His rags-to-riches story began when, at the age of 17, he launched his own auto salvage business after his dad died and he had no money and no place to live. He went on to build it into one of the largest operations of its kind in the United States.

In 1999, he sold his chain of salvage yards to Ford Motor Company. He repurchased what had become a money-losing business from Ford several years later. After whipping it back into profitability, Sturgeon and two partners sold it once more to Schnitzer Industries.

Today Sturgeon is a successful real estate investor and founder of Mr. Mission Possible small business consulting. He is also the founder of DFW Drive Your Dream exotic car driving experience, and the DFW Elite Toy Museum.

Sturgeon is the author of five business books including *Peer Benchmarking Groups, Green Weenies, How to Salvage*

Millions From Your Small Business, How to Salvage More Millions From Your Small Business, and *Getting to Yes With Your Banker. Pigs* is a dramatic departure for Sturgeon, the result of unleashing his analytical business skills on the riddle of male-female romantic relationships. It's a much-needed discussion that any red-blooded male (and female) will want to read.

A resident of Fort Worth, Texas, Sturgeon is the divorced father of three adult sons. After two years on the dating scene, he is currently in a successful, long-term romantic relationship with another entrepreneur. He attributes his romantic success to many of the principles he learned through his research for this book.

Send us your feedback and contributions to the Holy Grail List.

Comments? Reactions?
Post your feedback on the blog at
www.MenArePigsBook.com

The Holy Grail List is a Work in Progress
We're soliciting your ideas on which traits reveal those
women who NEED sex. What have we missed? Post
your suggestions to the Holy Grail list on the website.
If we accept your ideas, you can receive attribution plus
five free copies of the next edition of *Men are Pigs*.

Order Form

Online Orders: www.MenArePigsBook.com
E-Mail Orders: JenniferK@RDSInvestments.com
Fax Orders: (817) 838-8477
Phone Orders: (817) 834-3625, ext. 232
By Mail: 5940 Eden, Fort Worth Texas 76117

PRODUCTS:

Title	Price	Quantity	Subtotal
Men Are Pigs	$19.95	_____	_____
	Sales Tax*		_____
	Shipping & Handling**		_____
	TOTAL		_____

*Sales Tax: Please add 8.25% tax for products shipped to Texas addresses.
**Shipping and Handling: (US) Add $4 for first book and $2 for each additional book. Call for international pricing.

SHIPPING:

Name: _____

Address: _____

City, State Zip: _____

Telephone: _____

E-Mail Address: _____

PAYMENT:

❏ Check enclosed   ❏ VISA   ❏ MasterCard

Card Number: _____

Exp. Date: _____

Security Code: _____

Signature: _____

Name on card: _____

Billing Address: _____

City, State Zip: _____

GREAT BOOKS MAKE FANTASTIC GIFTS

Straightforward, illuminating, and highly rewarding, Ron Sturgeon's *Men Are Pigs* makes a thoughtful gift for a man or woman.

- *Men are Pigs* is packed with secrets, tools, and strategies for discovering those women who will satisfy a man's unique needs and desires—from mild to wild!

- *Men are Pigs* a powerful blueprint for building and rebuilding successful romantic relationships!

- *Men are Pigs* is a great resource for women who want to learn more about men, and how they can get what they want from their romantic relationships.

- *Men are Pigs* is a powerful tool for men to build satisfying relationships by giving all they've got to give to the *right* woman.

- *Men are Pigs* helps men and women understand each other: their similarities, their differences, and why it all works!

Quantity discounts available.
Order gift copies today by visiting

www.MenArePigsBook.com

or by contacting the publisher.